HIV INFECTION

HIV
INFECTION

THE FACTS

YOU NEED TO KNOW

KENNETH L. PACKER

98-193

VENTURE

FRANKLIN WATTS
A Division of Grolier Publishing
New York London Hong Kong Sydney
Danbury, Connecticut

Photographs ©:Imapress/Serge Attal, 51; Medichrome-The Stock Shop/Rick Brady, 23; Monkmeyer/Arlene Collins, 69; Monkmeyer/Randy Matusow, 59, 103; Monkmeyer/Bernard Wolf, 65; Hank Morgan, 89; Names Project, 133; Names Project Foundation/David Alosi & Ron Vak, 137; Names Project/Paul Margolies, 139; Kenneth L. Packer/Yvette, 130; Photo Researchers, Inc./Scott Camazine & Sue Trainor, 110; Rothco/Dick Adair, 15.

Visit Franklin Watts on the Internet at:
http://publishing.grolier.com

Interior Design by Claire Fontaine
Library of Congress Cataloging-in-Publication Data

Packer, Kenneth L.
    HIV infection: the facts you need to know / Kenneth L. Packer.
    p. cm. — (A Venture book)
    Includes bibliogra phical references and index.
    Summary: Explains HIV, how infection with it can lead to AIDS, how it is transmitted, and what is being done to prevent and cure the disease.

    ISBN 0-531-11333-7 (lib. bdg.)   0-531-15899-3 (pbk.)
    1. AIDS (Disease)—Juvenile literature.   [1. AIDS (Disease) 2. Diseases.] I. Title.
    RC607.A26P333 1998
    616.97'92—dc21   97-13755
                                                                 CIP
                                                                 AC

CONTENTS

DEDICATION

To my many AIDS education colleagues who have helped others practice the lowest level of risk-taking behavior that is acceptable to them; given their students the knowledge and skills to make a difference; helped others make sense out of an epidemic that makes no sense at all; given their clients hope for the future, and helped others treat HIV-positive people with dignity and compassion.

I want to thank Isabel Burk, Stephen Daniel, Ph.D., Jane Elven, Marjorie Fink, Tina Robi, and Dominick Splendorio—who generously gave their expertise, skill, and time toward the creation of this book.

A warm personal thanks to Yvette, who shared her life story, concerns, and feelings about HIV.

INTRODUCTION

HUMAN IMMUNODEFICIENCY VIRUS (HIV) INFECTION IS ONE of the most devastating diseases to touch the human race. Understanding its nature, transmission, and prevention is important for everyone, and it is only through education and skills that we can practice prevention.

This book has been written as a reference guide for teens and young adults. It is designed to answer your many questions and to help you research the information needed in your personal life or academic courses. Some will read the book from cover to cover; others will use it as a reference and look up specific information. For social studies students, it provides a history of the disease and an understanding of the socioeconomic impact of HIV on society. For humanities students, it provides an understanding of the devastation the disease has had on humans and the compassion needed for those infected and affected. For health education students, it provides an understanding of the importance of and techniques for prevention. For biology students, it provides information on the nature of the disease, the virus that causes it, and how it affects the function of the immune system. For peer leaders, it's a good source of information for peer counseling and education sessions. For all readers, it provides information and skills to help keep you disease free.

In chapter 9, a young woman living with HIV tells her story. She shows how the drug-using and sexual risks discussed in the book are very real. Her powerful story puts a face to HIV infection.

Unless *you* take action to prevent the spread of HIV, all this information won't do any good. The truth is, there's no reason that another person needs to become HIV-infected. We need only to take a good look at and maybe change our behavior, especially our sexual and drug-using behavior. Until a cure or vaccine is developed, maintaining safe behavior or changing unsafe behavior are the most effective ways to control the HIV epidemic.

A good way to begin thinking about HIV is to determine if you are at risk. Are you at risk of HIV infection? The checklist below will help you determine your level of risk. Don't write in this book. Instead, put the answers on a piece of paper. No one else has to look at your answers. They are as confidential as you want them to be. Be honest with yourself. Check every item that is true for you. Taking the test may raise questions about HIV and acquired immune deficiency syndrome (AIDS). You can look up the answers or discuss them with others.

The goal of HIV education is to empower individuals with the knowledge and skills necessary to practice the lowest level of risk-taking behavior. Be a messenger and get the prevention information out.

HIV Risk Survey

☐ 1. I have never had a sex partner.

☐ 2. I do not have intercourse but express intimacy in other ways.

☐ 3. I am in a new relationship, and neither my partner nor I have ever had sex with anyone else.

☒ 4. My partner and I have never shared needles.

☒ 5. My partner and I use a condom with a spermicide every time we have any kind of intercourse.

☐ 6. My partner and I have both been tested twice for HIV with negative result. Neither of us has shared needles for any purpose with anyone, and neither of us has any other sex partners.

☐ 7. I have sexual intercourse without using a condom or spermicide.

☐ 8. I have oral sex without using a condom or latex barrier.

☐ 9. I have sexual contact with someone whose sexual history is unknown to me.

☐ 10. I have sexual contact with someone who has had sex with many other partners.

☐ 11. I have sex with a man who has had sex with other men.

☐ 12. I have sex with someone whose needle-sharing history is unknown to me.

☐ 13. I share needles.

☐ 14. I had a blood transfusion between 1977 and 1985 or had sex with someone who had a blood transfusion during that time.

☐ 15. My use of drugs or alcohol sometimes leads me to have sexual encounters that I would like to forget.

Scoring:

▪ If you checked 1, 2, 3, or 4, you have almost no risk of HIV infection.

▪ If you checked 5 and 6, you have a low risk of HIV infection.

▪ If you checked 7, 8, 9, 10, 11, 12, 13, 14, or 15, you are at risk of HIV infection and should consider getting tested.

CHAPTER 1

THE
EPIDEMIC

WHEN AND WHERE DID HUMAN THE IMMUNODEFICIENCY virus (*HIV*) first appear? There's much speculation and research on this subject, and the truth is that no one really knows for sure.

HIV, the *virus* that causes *acquired immune deficiency syndrome* (*AIDS*), is a member of a family of viruses. The first member of this family, HTLV-I, was found in Africa, South America, and the Caribbean. It was related to STLV-I, a virus found in African monkeys. Researchers believe that both viruses came from a common ancestor in Africa.

Reports of an AIDS-like illness in central Africa dates to the early 1970s. *Antibodies* to this virus, HTLV-III, were found in stored African blood. This led to the speculation that HTLV-III originated in Africa. Most researchers agree that HTLV-III was a new strain of a very old virus. It is widespread in Uganda, Zaire, Rwanda, and other central African nations. In addition, a similar virus was found in the African green monkey. Several theories have been given on how the virus got into humans, but none of them have ever been proved. One theory is that people were bitten by infected monkeys.

Researchers believe that people infected with the virus left Africa and went to the Caribbean nation of Haiti. The virus then spread to the United States and the rest of the world.

Early Development of the Epidemic

The first cases of AIDS in the United States were reported in 1981. *Epidemiologists*, scientists who study the spread of *diseases*, at the Centers for Disease Control (CDC) in Atlanta, Georgia, began tracking the disease. They suspect that the first cases of AIDS in the United States occurred in the late 1970s.

These first U.S. cases were reported in homosexual men with many partners. The disease was, therefore, first known as *gay* cancer and then as gay related immune disorder (GRID). In 1981, the CDC was alerted to reports of cases of rare lung *infections*. These infections were all in previously healthy homosexual men in Los Angeles and New York City. It was *Pneumocystis carinii pneumonia*. This disease, caused by a *protozoan*, had previously caused pneumonia only in patients with poor immune defenses.

Later, cases of a rare tumor, *Kaposi's sarcoma*, were reported in young homosexual men. Kaposi's sarcoma is a slow-growing skin cancer previously seen in Africa and in the United States in elderly men. In cases of AIDS, however, the cancer was much more aggressive. It was found in other parts of the body besides the skin.

These collective reports rang the alarm of a new *syndrome*, a group of *signs* and *symptoms* of a disease. At that time, scientists and physicians did not really know what it

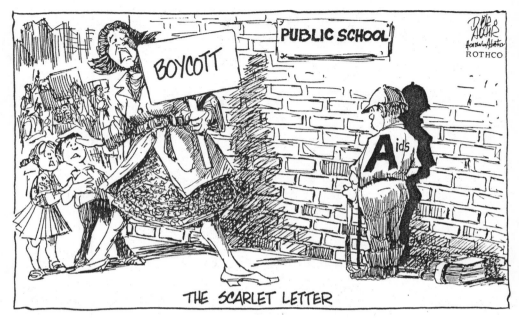

THE SCARLET LETTER

This cartoon comments on the hysteria that surrounded AIDS in the 1980s.

was. What was alarming was how fast it was spreading and that there was no cure. As a result, there was much irrational behavior and fear of those who were HIV-infected.

In cities all across the United States, homosexuals felt the impact of AIDS. They and their families watched as friends and loved ones got sick and died. This story repeated itself countless times. Many were asking why this was happening. What was the cause? Why wasn't the government doing more? Was it because most of those early cases of infected people were gay, black, or poor? Would the response be different if those infected were from mainstream America?

By late 1981, AIDS had been reported in intravenous drug users who had shared needles to inject drugs. Then in mid-1982, the first AIDS cases were noted in *hemophiliacs*. Shortly after that, AIDS was diagnosed in patients who had received *blood transfusions*. Cases were then found in sexual partners of infected individuals.

AIDS cases continued to rise, and by the end of 1982, they had been reported in 15 states, the District of Columbia, and two more countries. At that time, scientists had very little information about the disease. They still didn't know what it was. The following year, the size of the problem became clear. By December 1983, a total of 3,000 cases had been reported in 42 states, the District of Columbia, and 20 other countries. By the end of 1985, the number of reported cases would increase to a total of 16,000 and would continue to rise at an uncontrolled rate.

In 1983, French and American researchers identified the responsible virus. The virus was named LAV (lymphadenopathy-associated virus) by the French scientist, Luc Montagnier of the Pasteur Institute. The same virus was named HTLV-III (human T-cell lymphotropic virus strain III) by the American scientist, Robert Gallo of the U.S. National Institutes of Health. In 1986, it was renamed HIV (human immunodeficiency virus).

With no cure in sight, authorities agreed that the only hope was prevention education. Education was needed in schools, and community awareness was needed for parents and the general public. The issue of education has posed many dilemmas and sparked debates that remain ongoing. The primary dilemma for American culture was how to discuss HIV prevention without talking about sex.

Most schools had little or no comprehensive sex education. Do we teach students about *abstinence* only and ignore that most people will be sexually active sometime in their lives? If this is to be prevention, then they need to know about it beforehand, not after it is too late. Do we teach real skills for HIV prevention, like condom-use skills, negotiating skills, needle-cleaning skills, refusal skills, and self-esteem skills, or do we just say no?

By December 1986, the initial *transmission* patterns of the disease in the United States became clear: 66 percent in *homosexual* and bisexual men (men having sex with men and women); 24 percent in *IV drug* users; 1 percent in persons with *hemophilia*; 4 percent in *heterosexual* partners of high-risk persons; 2 percent from blood transfusions; and 3 percent other.[1] (The "other" category designated individuals who did not have enough information to determine the cause.) Over time, these categories have remained on the list, and only the percentage of each group has changed.

As the number of cases rose, so did the level of hysteria. People were fired from their jobs because they were HIV-infected. Students were forced into homebound instruction for fear they would infect others in the classroom. Some medical professionals refused to treat HIV-positive individuals for fear of contracting the disease. Insurance companies mandated testing for new customers, the military rejected anyone who was infected, and families with an HIV-infected member were harassed and driven out of schools and communities.

Through December 1995, the CDC reported that 2,354 adolescents (13 to 19 years of age) and 18,955 young adults (20 to 24 years of age) had been reported with AIDS. In 1995 alone, 405 adolescents and 2,432 young adults were reported with new AIDS cases. In that year almost 1 in 5 AIDS cases were diagnosed in the 20-to-29 year-old age group. Because of the often long time between infection and development of AIDS, many of these persons were likely infected as teenagers. Estimates based on the age distribution of AIDS cases suggest that in future years as many as half the new HIV infections may be among people under age 25.

Among adolescents reported with AIDS, older teens, males, and racial ethnic minorities have been disproportionately affected. The percentage of females reported with AIDS has increased over time. In 1995, 40 percent of adolescents reported with AIDS were female. The majority of AIDS cases among youth are attributed to *sexual contact*. Among male adolescents and young adults (ages 13–24), 60 percent were attributed to male-to-male sex and 3 percent to heterosexual contact.

From 1986 to December 1996, the pattern of HIV infection in the United States took on a different look. Heterosexual individuals, especially women and teens, were the group of persons with AIDS that increased the fastest. The infection data from the end of 1996 showed this pattern: 44 percent in homosexual and bisexual men; 26 percent in IV drug users; 9 percent in men with multiple risks; 1 percent in persons with hemophilia; 12 percent in heterosexual individuals; 1 percent from blood transfusions; 7 percent other (no risks reported).[2]

The Spread of the Disease

As of mid-1993, more than 14 million people worldwide were believed to have been infected with the virus. HIV infection is now found in every country of the world. It is truly *pandemic*, meaning that it's a disease epidemic that has spread around the world. Data from around the world show similarities and differences regarding the spread of the disease. In Africa and the Caribbean, HIV infection spread mainly through heterosexual contact (sex between males and females). Then bisexual individuals (persons who have sex with both men and women) spread it to the homosexual population.

In North and South America, Europe, and Australia, the

disease is believed to have started with homosexual men. It then spread to bisexual men and then to *intravenous* drug users who share needles to inject drugs. It was finally spread to heterosexual individuals from the bisexual men and heterosexual drug users. Now the disease is being spread from one heterosexual person to another.

At the beginning of the epidemic, more men than women in developed countries were infected with HIV. This was because of the initial male homosexual spread of the disease. As heterosexual transmission became more common, the difference in rates between men and women shrank. In Africa, where the majority of people with HIV live, more women are infected than men. In 1993, there were three men infected for every two women worldwide. The World Health Organization predicts that by the year 2000, infections among women will almost equal the number of infected men worldwide.

As the number of cases in women has increased, so has the number of children born with HIV. An estimated one million have been infected through mother-to-child transmission. Most of these children develop AIDS and often die by age six. Others live longer, and with new medications and treatments, more are surviving to adolescence.

Other Epidemics

Many so-called plagues have been described in ancient history. The details are not clear, but the first recorded epidemic may have taken place in 3180 B.C. in Egypt. The Old Testament includes accounts of several plagues and illnesses. In the Middle Ages, the black death killed thousands.

Bubonic Plague
The bubonic plague, known in the past as the black death or black plague, infects wild rodents and is transmitted by

the rat flea. Most people become infected from domestic rats. Overcrowding and poor sanitation provides an opportunity for the rat fleas to bite humans. Although the fleas prefer rats as a host, they will live on humans.

The flea becomes infected when it bites an infected host. The organism grows in the flea's intestine. When the flea bites another person, it regurgitates infected fluid into the person and spreads the disease. Humans often spread the disease to other people when the plague victim develops pneumonia. The disease is then spread in the air from droplet infection during coughing.

At least three epidemics of the bubonic plague have occurred. The first was recorded in the sixth century A.D. The second was in the 14th century. The last was in the late 19th century.

The black plague had devastating effects. It caused large swellings on the groin and under the arms that oozed blood and pus. Boils spread over the body, black blotches covered the skin, and patients vomited and coughed up blood. The plague spread rapidly, killing 90 percent of its victims. Most died within a week. Graveyards filled fast, so people were often buried in mass graves.

Ignorance increased the terror of the disease. Some in the Middle Ages blamed it on astrology (that is, the alignment of Saturn, Jupiter, and Mars in the fourth degree of Aquarius). Many believed that God sent the plague as a punishment, repeating the story of Moses and the Egyptians. Others blamed demons and spirits. Christians massacred thousands of Jews, believing they had contaminated Christian wells. Physicians could not help, having no cure or understanding of the disease. People isolated themselves and even abandoned their sick children. This fear and ignorance can be equated to some of the similar behavior at the beginning of the HIV epidemic.

Cholera

Cholera is an intestinal disease caused by a bacteria. It causes severe diarrhea and vomiting, which can rapidly produce potentially fatal dehydration if untreated. A cholera epidemic killed millions of people in the 1800s. Before it was discovered that the disease was caused by contaminated water, people thought it was caused by evil, supernatural forces. Peasants in Hungary rioted when they thought the rich were using forces that caused the disease against them. Finally, John Snow, an Englishman, discovered the cause and helped people to realize the importance of proper sanitation and unpolluted water.

Influenza

The influenza epidemic of 1918 was one of the worst in history. More than 40 million people worldwide were killed. In San Francisco, everyone was required to wear a surgical mask.

Polio

Caused by a virus, polio is a disease that causes paralysis by attacking the spinal cord. It mainly affects children. A polio epidemic struck in the 1940s. Pools, movie theaters, and other public places were closed, and children were quarantined. Some died. Others were crippled. The polio epidemic ended with the advent of the Salk polio *vaccine*. The initial fear and isolation of polio patients is akin to the ways in which AIDS patients were treated early on in the epidemic.

Syphilis

Syphilis was first detected in Europe, where it had been brought back by sailors on their return from the Americas. It first appeared in Spain in 1493 and in Italy around 1497. From there, it spread throughout Europe. As in other epidemics, where knowledge of the disease was minimal, there was much blaming. The French blamed the Italians, and the Italians blamed the French.

Like HIV infection, syphilis starts as a mild condition with few symptoms. In this case, nonpainful sores (chancres) appear. This is followed by a latent stage with no symptoms. In the second stage, there is inflammation of the skin, eyes, liver, heart, and the central nervous system. The third stage of syphilis causes tumors or lesions in the heart and aorta. Death is the final stage. For almost 400 years there was no treatment or cure for syphilis. As a result, the death rate was high from massive bleeding or nervous system destruction.

There are many parallels between the AIDS epidemic and the syphilis epidemic. Both HIV and syphilis take several years to develop, are transmitted sexually, and destroy the nervous system. Both have caused suspicion, blame, and hysteria. Luckily, syphilis is now curable with penicillin or other *antibiotics*. HIV infection, however, is not.

The Safety of the Blood Supply

The blood supply plays a critical role in the world health system. The issues of blood safety and AIDS have been interrelated since the beginning of the epidemic. No country stands alone, because blood is often transported across boundaries to alleviate shortages. Although the blood supply today is the safest it has ever been, blood and blood products are not completely risk free. There is a very small risk of infection with HIV and *hepatitis*, as well as *blood typing* problems. Before March 1985, a significant number of people became HIV infected from blood *transfusions*.

A blood transfusion is when another person's blood is used to replace blood you have lost or need. You may have lost it due to an accident or during surgery. Transfusions or

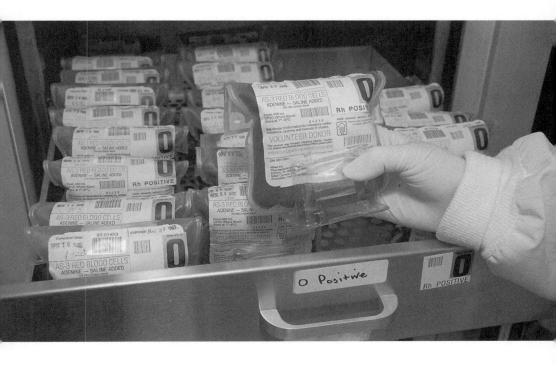

A blood bank worker holds a pint of blood. Blood banks now test donated blood for HIV contamination.

blood products may also be needed to correct medical conditions, such as a hemophiliac needing blood-clotting factor. Unfortunately, many hemophiliacs received contaminated clotting factor in the years before the blood was properly tested.

Today, blood products, such as immune globulin and clotting factors, are treated to destroy any virus. *Blood banks* and laboratories use a variety of methods—including heat, solvents, or detergents—to make the blood safe. All blood and *blood donors* are tested for HIV. This has stopped the infection of hemophiliacs and others from the blood products they need to survive.

Before March 1985, not every blood donor was tested for HIV. This situation changed when it was realized that the blood supply was contaminated with HIV from infected donors. Now, all blood donors are asked questions about their medical, drug-using, and sexual history and are tested for HIV. If blood tests or questionnaires show that a person's blood might be infected, it will not be used or stored in the blood bank. The chances of blood being HIV-contaminated are small. Whatever that risk may be, for those that need blood transfusions it is far less than the risk of dying or becoming seriously ill without the transfusion.

Contaminated blood might get through the screening process for two reasons. Donors might not tell the truth about their history or might unknowingly be in the window period. Research has shown that most people tell the truth before giving blood. Many of those that do not are given a second chance with the question, "Would you rather have your blood given to a patient or used for research?" That allows a person to indicate there is a problem without saying it directly.

It is important *not* to give blood as a way to get tested, as some have done in the past. Testing is free at most government-funded clinics. If you donate to get tested and don't tell of your risk, that blood may slip through.

Researchers have estimated that the chance of blood being contaminated with HIV is now 1 in 225,000 units. The risk of hepatitis B is 1 in 250,000, and the risk for hepatitis C is 1 in 3,300. A person can improve the chances of getting noninfected blood by using his or her own blood for elective surgery. This is known as self-donation, or *autologous transfusion.* The blood is stored for self-use. Even self-use blood is tested for HIV, hepatitis, and other diseases.

CHAPTER 2

THE IMMUNE SYSTEM

HIV IS AN EFFICIENT INVADER. IT CAN DESTROY THE BODY'S *immune system*, which is supposed to counteract a disease invasion. Because HIV can disable the immune system, it attacks the body like no other organism.

Usually, the skin, the cilia (small, hairlike structures) lining the trachea, and the intestines act as effective barriers. They keep back many invading organisms. Those that get through these barriers are attacked by immune system cells.

A good immune response depends on the immune system cells coordinating their attack. HIV cripples the immune system by destroying some of these immune system cells. In doing this, HIV is then safe from the immune system. It can live and reproduce in the body. In addition, with the immune system disabled, the body cannot fight other diseases. Thus, people with AIDS, the end stage of HIV infection (see chapter 4), suffer from *opportunistic infec-*

tions—infections that would normally be eliminated by the healthy immune system in a healthy person.

Immune system cells each have very special jobs. Some eliminate *bacteria* and viruses. Others check for and remove cancerous cells. Still others neutralize toxins or poisons in the body. Finally, others regulate the system by starting and stopping the immune system cells and their functions.

Cells of the Immune System

Cells of the immune system can be grouped by function. Some cells become first-response cells. Some are killer cells. Others are debris eaters. Some become memory cells.

B Cells

Mature *B cells* are responsible for antibody (a substance that fights infection) production. On recognition of a foreign *antigen*, an invader in the body, B cells expand in number. They secrete large quantities of antibodies that float freely in the blood. They are not attached to the B cell. These antibodies have surface receptors that recognize a specific antigen or invader. The high level of circulating antibodies bind to the antigen and help remove it from the body. Some B cells do not actively secrete antibodies. They become memory cells, which keep the system ready to respond if the antigen comes back several months later.

T Cells

Like B cells, *T cells* remain in the blood for many years after an antigen attack. T cells have different jobs:

- T lymphocytes destroy cells foreign to the body.
- Suppressor T cells turn off B-cell and T-cell function when their work is no longer needed.

How B Cells Function

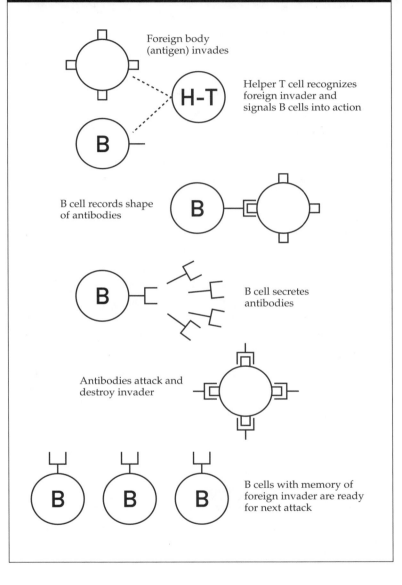

Foreign body (antigen) invades

Helper T cell recognizes foreign invader and signals B cells into action

B cell records shape of antibodies

B cell secretes antibodies

Antibodies attack and destroy invader

B cells with memory of foreign invader are ready for next attack

- Helper T cells regulate the activity of the B cells, T cells, and other cells in the immune system.

- Inducer T cells support the growth and production of T cells and B cells.

T cells have surface *proteins* called CD4 sites. The CD4 surface protein and another cell part, the T-cell antigen receptor (CTR), enable the T cell to bind with its target invader. These binding sites stay attached to the T cell. They are neither secreted nor free floating, like the antibodies produced by the B cell. These sites allow T cells to recognize antigens, kill them, or help other cells do their job. T cells travel throughout the body patrolling for foreign invaders.

Macrophage Cells

The macrophage is a highly mobile cell. It has CD4 sites, and it can bind to almost any antigen. Macrophages work by surrounding and absorbing the antigen. They also give pieces of the antigen to the T cells. The T cells use these pieces to build CTR sites on their surface. Macrophages, therefore, serve as a surveillance and immune system building function.

Monocytes, another type of white blood cell, can penetrate body tissue. They then grow into macrophages. Monocytes do their work inside tissues instead of in body fluid, like B cells and T cells.

Dendritic Cells

Dendritic cells are white blood cells. They are found in small numbers in the skin, lymph nodes, spleen, and mucosal tissue. They alert circulating T cells to the presence of antigens, thereby starting the immune response. Although few in number, dendritic cells are very effective.

M Cells

M cells are found on the surface of the intestinal and rectal mucosa. They have highly specialized surveillance structures. M cells bring invading antigens to lymph tissue, where the immune response can be started.

Natural Killer Cells

Natural killer cells work by poking holes into target cells. These targets are body cells that have become infected or cancerous. Killer cells detect any abnormal cell and get rid of it.

The Normal Immune Response

An important ability of the immune system is to know the difference between "me" and "not me" (what belongs in the body and what does not). This ability is learned by the immune system during fetal development. Only T cells recognize invaders as "not me." B cells do not recognize a new invader unless signaled by an activated helper T cell.

Once signaled, the B cells produce floating antibodies and act as memory cells for future invasions. The signal of an invasion also causes other things to happen. Macrophages, dendritic cells, and natural killer cells carry out their functions. B cells continue to produce antibodies and memory cells. Immune cells signal or communicate with each other by releasing chemicals called *cytokines*. As the invasion diminishes, suppressor T cells respond to stop the immune reaction. Without this, the body would be overwhelmed with immune cells and antibodies. After an initial invasion, certain B cells and T cells remember what the invader looks like. They are ready to fight again if another invasion occurs.

Vaccines are usually an injection given to people to prevent a disease. They work by faking an invasion of a disease. Vaccines are usually made of killed or weakened bacteria or virus. Some newer vaccines are made of synthetic products produced in a laboratory. They cause the immune system to react and produce antibodies and memory cells without the person being sick. Because it is not a real attack, the numbers of foreign particles are small, and they cannot reproduce. Therefore, people sometimes need boosters or extra shots to continue the immune response. (See chapter 7, Vaccine Development.)

The Immune System Under HIV Attack

Recent research has revealed many secrets of the immune system. Under the normal circumstances of most viral attacks, the immune system would eliminate the invader. Memory cells would be ready for future attacks.

With HIV infection, the virus gets around the immune system. It does this by attacking the very cells designed to protect the body. HIV also changes shape, thereby escaping detection, and it can hide inside cells avoiding detection.

Target Cells for HIV Infection

HIV is attracted to certain immune cells. Those are the cells with CD4 receptor sites. This happens because HIV has an envelope protein called gp120 that is attracted to the CD4 site. Some of these CD4 cells act as reservoirs for HIV to hide in. Others become factories for HIV to reproduce itself. Immune system cells that serve HIV in these ways include helper T cells, macrophages, monocytes, and dendritic cells. In addition, other body cells—placental cells, bone marrow cells, small intestine and colon cells, vascular endothelial cells (cells around blood vessels), and cells of the thymus gland—have been suspected of acting as reservoirs for HIV to hide in, but more research is needed to prove this theory.

Destruction of Immune Cells

The main effect of HIV infection is the depletion of CD4 cells. This happens in several ways. Replication of the virus can kill the cells. Stuffing the cell with budding viruses can break the cell. Replication of the virus can use up nutrients and particles in the cell, thus starving it to death. Others self-destruct when they realize they are defective from changes in *DNA* caused by HIV. (DNA is a double strand of genetic material and contains the inherited traits of an organism.) Natural killer cells may recognize the CD4 cells as infected and destroy them. Finally, CD4 cells are killed when they clump together to form a multinucleated mass (many cells hooked together) called a *syncytia*.

Altered Surface of HIV

The ability of HIV to escape immune system destruction is mostly due to its ability to change appearance. It is a master at altering the look of its surface proteins. With each change of structure comes renewed ability to avoid detection. In addition, the antibodies made for the original-shaped virus now no longer work. This ability to change shape is known as *heterogeneity*. Researchers have documented the changes that occur within HIV in a single individual as the disease progresses. They have also found that HIV in different body locations sometimes has different surfaces or different shapes.

Immune System Response To HIV Attack

HIV gradually destroys the immune system. During early infection, however, the immune system mounts a vigorous attack on the virus. This early response is the same as a response to any other virus. All immune system cells and parts carry out their expected roles. The strength and length of this first immune response may define the length of the *asymptomatic* phase (a time of no symptoms) of HIV infection. Recent research has shown that early and quick T-cell responses to HIV help prevent short-term impairment of the central nervous system. Unfortunately, it also is an indicator of eventual faster disease progression.

HIV infection triggers a massive mobilization of B cells. These B cells secrete large amounts of antibodies. These antibodies go to work targeting free-floating viruses and getting macrophages to remove them. Killer T cells identify infected cells and destroy them by poking tiny holes in the cell membrane. They also work to prevent early replication of the virus. Unfortunately this early response is not enough to prevent the destruction of the immune system.

Helper T cells start to work almost as soon as infection occurs. This response may begin in many infected individuals even before antibodies are detected. Once people become *seropositive* (the point when antibodies can be detected in the blood), much of the T-cell response is lost.

In healthy individuals, a large loss of immune cells is usually counteracted by the bone marrow producing new cells. This is the case during radiation or chemotherapy for cancer treatment. The bone marrow can repopulate the immune cells within a few months' time. Why does this not happen with immune cell destruction from HIV? It seems that HIV infects the immune-producing cells of the bone marrow. This prevents them from producing more immune cells.

As HIV infection progresses, cytokine (chemicals that cause other things to happen) production becomes upset. Normal cytokine production stimulates positive immune system responses. Instead, cells infected with HIV produce cytokines that attract uninfected CD4 cells to the area. These CD4 cells become infected. Some of these cytokines stimulate HIV to replicate inside infected cells.

To make matters worse, the HIV infection response often produces massive numbers of antibodies. As the pool of antibodies becomes very large, the antibodies' ability to tell the difference between "me" and "not me" is lost. Some antibodies start attacking the body's cells. So the virus can use the immune system and its parts to grow and reproduce.

CHAPTER 3

THE VIRUS

HIV IS ONE OF THE MOST ADAPTABLE VIRUSES EVER FOUND. Scientists have described it as a stealth invader, an elusive target, and a devious disguiser. Its genetic control system makes it a formidable opponent, but as the knowledge of HIV has increased, so has the ability to deal with it.

HIV: A Retrovirus

HIV is classified as an *RNA* (ribonucleic acid) virus because its genetic information is contained in RNA. (RNA is a single strand of genetic material that contains inherited traits.) It belongs to the *retrovirus* family, which have several features in common. They:

- have two single strands of RNA

- have a membrane-like outer cover known as an envelope

- reproduce or replicate using DNA
- hide themselves in the DNA of the host cell

Retroviruses must convert their RNA to DNA. This conversion is called reverse transcription, or retrotransmission. Reverse transcription is necessary for replication (reproduction). It also enables the retrovirus to use the protein-making ability of the host cell. Through the process of integration, the viruses' genetic material starts to look like that of the host. Retroviruses are unusual because the are the only type of virus that associates their DNA with the host cell DNA.

Retroviruses first make a DNA copy of their RNA. Then a second copy is made. The double strand of DNA is incorporated in the host cell's DNA. When the host cell replicates its genetic material, it also replicates the viral genetic material. In this way, the virus uses the host cell as a factory to produce its genetic material, allowing more viruses to be produced.

Structure of HIV

HIV has a very simple structure. It is a membrane of proteins that contains genetic material inside. The parts are shown in the diagram on page 36. Notice that each part has not only a name but also a reference number, such as gp41 or p7.

Envelope Protein
An outside sheath, or envelope, serves as a protective membrane. On this envelope are glycoproteins, molecules of sugar and protein, that give the virus its bumpy look. Each bump has two glycoproteins. One is a top protein (gp120), and the other is a stemlike structure, a transmembrane glycoprotein (gp41).

Human Immunodeficiency Virus (HIV)

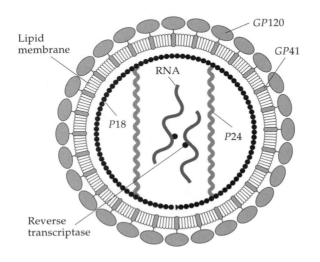

Lipid membrane

GP120

GP41

RNA

P18

P24

Reverse transcriptase

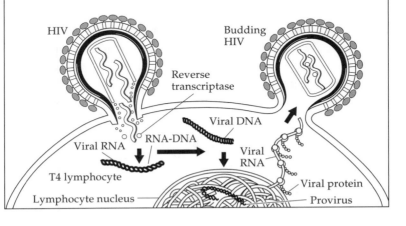

HIV

Budding HIV

Reverse transcriptase

Viral DNA

Viral RNA   RNA-DNA

Viral RNA

T4 lymphocyte

Viral protein

Lymphocyte nucleus

Provirus

Inner Shell

An inner shell, or matrix protein (p17), lies beneath the envelope. It is attached to the envelope.

Core

HIV has a core of capsid protein (p24). It surrounds the genetic information and nucleic acid protein (p7).

RNA

HIV's genetic material is RNA. The RNA is present as two single strands that contain the genes with codes for the viral proteins, viral *enzymes*, and regulatory proteins of HIV.

Enzymes

All retroviruses have three enzymes: reverse transcriptase, integrase, and protease. These enzymes help with retroviral replication in the host cell. Reverse transcriptase helps in the building of a single strand of DNA that is a copy of HIV RNA. It also destroys the original RNA molecule as the new DNA is made.

Entry of HIV into Other Host Cells

The HIV surface is covered by bumpy structures (gp120). These bumps are the "key" in a lock-and-key relationship that hooks HIV to a host cell. The "lock" is a structure on the host cell known as a CD4 receptor. Immune system cells have these CD4 receptors. After HIV and the host cell hook together, the virus fuses with the host cell.

Growth of New HIV

Through a building process inside the host cell, new HIV RNA is produced. Once inside the host cell, the core protein

Diagram of HIV Entering Cell and Reproducing

CD4-Cell attacked by HIV

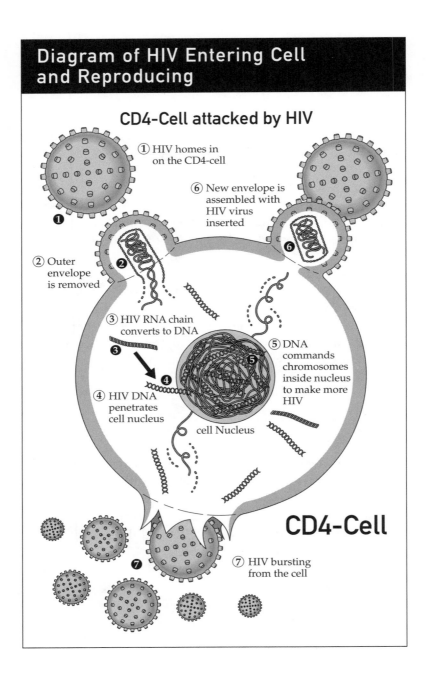

① HIV homes in on the CD4-cell

⑥ New envelope is assembled with HIV virus inserted

❶

② Outer envelope is removed

❷

③ HIV RNA chain converts to DNA

❸

❹

④ HIV DNA penetrates cell nucleus

⑤ DNA commands chromosomes inside nucleus to make more HIV

❺

cell Nucleus

❻

CD4-Cell

❼

⑦ HIV bursting from the cell

is shed, and RNA transcription to DNA takes place. HIV proteins and the HIV RNA are assembled near the cell membrane. Parts of the host cell membrane are used to form the viral envelope and finally a new HIV buds from the host cell.

Different Strains of HIV

Researchers have identified three different strains, or types, of HIV.

HIV-1

Technically, our discussion of HIV has been about HIV-1. This is the strain found in most of the world. HIV-1, however, has many substrains of the virus. Each substrain has a slightly different genetic makeup. These minor changes are used to the virus's advantage, allowing it to look different to the body's immune system in its attempt to attack it. These changes, however, are so minor that the variations are still considered the same virus. In the same way, some people have blue eyes and some have brown, but are all human beings.

HIV-2

In 1985, a second HIV virus, *HIV-2*, was found in a Portuguese man living in the Cape Verde Islands. He had symptoms resembling those of AIDS patients, but he did not clearly test positive for HIV. Tests have now been developed to detect HIV-2. In fact, in many locations the test is done when checking for HIV-1. HIV-2 is found mostly in West Africa.

SIV

The simian immunodeficiency virus (SIV) is found in wild monkeys in Africa. These species include green, sooty mangabeys, mandrills, and patas monkeys. These monkeys are all carriers of the virus but do not show disease symptoms. On the other hand, such Asian monkeys as the rhesus macaque are not infected in the wild. When they are exposed to SIV they do become ill with simian AIDS (SAIDS).

There is speculation that SIV might have somehow infected humans and then mutated into HIV as we know it today, but this connection has not been proved. Much research is being done in this area. If we learn the exact evolution of HIV, clues may be found to its cure or elimination. Knowing exactly why SIV does not produce disease symptoms in some monkeys may also give clues to a cure.

Retroviruses in Other Species

Retroviruses have also been found in animals other than monkeys and humans.

Cats
Two retroviruses infect cats. The first is feline leukemia virus (FeLV), which is an oncovirus (tumor-causing virus). The second is feline immunodeficiency virus (FIV), which is very similar to HIV in symptoms and progression of the infection. The cats develop swollen *lymph glands*, opportunistic infections, and brain dysfunction. Both viruses are prevalent worldwide but infect only cats. They are not a threat to humans.

Cattle
Retroviruses infect cattle. Bovine immunodeficiency virus (BIV) causes an AIDS-like disease. Like cats, cattle are also infected by an oncovirus, bovine leukemia virus (BLV). These viruses do not infect humans, even when the meat of an infected animal is eaten.

CHAPTER 4

FROM HIV TO AIDS

IN THE EARLY YEARS WHEN THIS DISEASE WAS FIRST discovered, people were only thinking about the illness AIDS. But if you only think about AIDS, you miss an entire stage of the disease. More correctly, the disease of concern is HIV infection. AIDS is the end stage of HIV infection. A person can be HIV positive—meaning that he or she has HIV infection—without having AIDS. In this chapter we will clear up the confusion and describe the progression of the disease.

Disease Progression

HIV infection is a chronic (continuing over a long time), progressive (continually getting worse) disease. It destroys the immune system and produces a wide range of symptoms. These symptoms can be different from patient to patient. The progress of the disease, however, tends to advance in

Continuum of HIV Infection

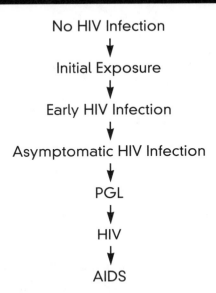

No HIV Infection
↓
Initial Exposure
↓
Early HIV Infection
↓
Asymptomatic HIV Infection
↓
PGL
↓
HIV
↓
AIDS

HIV for most patients follows a continuum of stages. The exact symptoms in each person may be different. The length of time it takes to progress from one stage to the next will vary with each patient. The length of time is influenced by many cofactors.

distinct stages. The rate of progress from stage to stage varies from person to person.

Stages of HIV Infection

The first stage of HIV infection is the *initial exposure*. Exposure to HIV can be from sexual contact, needle sharing or other blood exposure, or from mother to infant.

About three to six weeks after exposure to HIV, many individuals develop a flulike illness. This is the *early HIV infection* stage. It is also called the acute stage. These flulike symptoms can range from mild to very severe. This stage lasts from 3 to 14 days and sometimes longer. Everyone gets the flu and expects to be ill at some time or another. Therefore, the symptoms are often taken for granted. In fact, only about 30 percent of HIV patients can recall their early flu-like symptoms.

As with the flu, the symptoms, as bad as they may be, do go away. Because of the devastating nature of the disease and its association with sex and drugs, there is great denial—denial of the risk, denial of the symptoms, and denial one might be infected. That the first flulike symptoms go away reinforces the denial. A person thinks, "See there is nothing wrong with me, I just had a bad case of the flu."

When the flu-like symptoms disappear, the person enters the next stage, the asymptomatic stage. At this time there are no symptoms, and the person looks and feels perfectly healthy. This asymptomatic stage can last for 10 years or longer. Unfortunately, during early HIV infection and the asymptomatic stage, the disease can be highly infectious. This is because of high levels of virus in the person's body. They can transmit HIV to another person through sexual contact, needle sharing, or by their blood getting directly into another person's body in some way.

When the asymptomatic stage ends, the flulike symptoms return. This time, however, large swollen glands are usually the most pronounced symptom. For that reason the stage is often called the PGL (persistent generalized lymphadenopathy) stage. This stage lasts from three months to a year and sometimes longer.

The final stage is AIDS. Unfortunately there is no cure, no immunity, and no vaccine. The average life expectancy from time of AIDS diagnosis to death is about three years. Some live longer; some die sooner. The good news is that with new medical treatments, more patients are living longer.

Symptoms of HIV Infection

1. Swollen lymph glands in neck, armpits, or groin

2. Nightsweats, fever, chills

3. Non-dieting weight loss (10 or more pounds)

4. Extreme tiredness, fatigue

5. Long lasting diarrhea

6. Dry hacking cough

7. Thrush (white coating on tongue or inside mouth)

8. Peristent low grade fever

9. Short term memory loss

10. Rapid mood changes

11. Purple, pink, or black spots or bumps on skin

Factors Affecting Disease Progression

In 1990, scientists studied 489 men from San Francisco. They were selected for the research study because all had known dates of *seroconversion*. Researchers studied how long it took these men to progress to a diagnosis of AIDS. Within two years 1 percent had progressed; within four years, 8 percent;

within 10 years, 51 percent; and within 11 years, 54 percent (cumulative percentages). Why did some progress faster than others? It seems there are variations within individuals plus different *cofactors* in their lives. Studies have shown that the presence of certain cofactors speed the progression of the disease.

Age
Several studies have shown that age is important. The older an adult is at the time of infection, the faster the disease progresses. This has been shown to be true among hemophiliacs and drug users who are HIV positive. The disease, however, progresses faster in infants than in young adults.

Cigarette Smoking
Several studies have shown that smoking increases the progression rate of HIV infection. It stresses the body and the immune system. Fighting off infection is therefore harder for a smoker.

Alcohol and Other Drugs
Use of alcohol; other drugs, including caffeine; and such substances as sugar also damages the immune response and may hasten progression.

Viral Strains
There are several strains of HIV. Some are more virulent, or deadly, than others. In fact, the virus itself changes, sometimes to a more virulent form. Viruses in asymptomatic individuals tend to be less virulent than viruses found in people with AIDS.

Socioeconomic Factors
Economically disadvantaged individuals tend to progress faster toward AIDS. They have less access to medical care

and medications and often live in rundown, less sanitary conditions. They may also have suffered years of poor nutrition and high *stress*.

Psychological Factors

Positive mental and spiritual health tend to slow the progression of the disease. Conversely, depression in patients tends to speed up the disease. Those who practice *stress management*, meditation, and relaxation often have a slower progression of the disease.[1]

Wellness

Those who practice good wellness techniques have a slower progression of the disease. These techniques include daily exercise; good nutrition, special diets, and weight control; non-use of drugs, alcohol, and tobacco; and regular visits to the doctor, taking an active role in health care, and following medical advice.

A Definition of AIDS

A person can be HIV positive and still not have AIDS. Because this is true, at what moment does a patient get a diagnosis of AIDS? As researchers learned more about the disease, the answer to this question has changed several times since the early 1980s.

The original case definition of AIDS included patients with a depressed immune system who had at least one illness tied to the HIV syndrome. An alternate definition included patients who, in addition to a depressed immune system, had a positive HIV antibody test and at least one disease from a list of infections. It was later changed again to include brain dysfunction (*dementia*) and HIV wasting

Conditions Included in The 1993 AIDS Surveillance Case Definition

Candidiasis of bronchi, trachea, or lungs

Candidiasis, esophageal

Cervical cancer, invasive

Coccidioidomycosis, disseminated or extrapulmonary

Cryptococcosis, extrapulmonary

Cryptosporidiosis, chronic intestinal (>1 month's duration)

Cytomegalovirus disease (other than liver, spleen, or nodes)

Cytomegalovirus retinitis (with loss of vision)

Encephalopathy, HIV-related

Herpes simplex: chronic ulcer(s) (>1 month's duration); or bronchitis, pneumonitis, or esophagitis

Histoplasmosis, disseminated or extrapulmonary

Isosporiasis, chronic intestinal (>1 month's duration)

Kaposi's sarcoma

Lymphoma, Burkitt's (or equivalent term)

Lymphoma, immunoblastic (or equivalent term)

Lymphoma, primary, or brain

Mycobacterium avium complex or M. kansasii, disseminated or extrapulmonary

Mycobacterium tuberculosis, any site (pulmonary or extrapulmonary)

Mycobacterium, other species or unidentified species, disseminated or extrapulmonary

Pneumocystis carinii pneumonia

Pneumonia, recurrent

Progressive multifocal leukoencephalopathy

Salmonella septicemia, recurrent

Toxoplasmosis of the brain

Wasting syndrome due to HIV

Source: "1993 Revised Classification System for HIV Infection and Expanded Surveillance Case Definitions for AIDS Among Adolescents and Adults," MMWR, vol. 41, no. RR-l7, Centers for Disease Control and Prevention, Atlanta, GA, December 18, 1992.

syndrome (where a person with AIDS loses a great deal of weight and muscle, looking like skin and bones). In 1987, the definition was revised again to include a longer list of diseases found in a person with HIV infection.

With each of these changes more people were included in the definition. The disease in the United States, where a large part of the early AIDS research was done, was first identified in the male homosexual population. Therefore, the research and definitions were created based on that population. As the disease spread to other groups—African-Americans, Hispanics, injection drug users, and women—new definitions were needed because these groups were showing different symptoms and different opportunistic infections.

In 1993, the definition was totally revised. Because the disease spread to the heterosexual population, it was infecting more women. Pelvic inflammatory disease, candidiasis (a *sexually transmitted disease*), and cervical cancer were becoming common in women with advanced HIV infection. Because these diseases were not on the list of opportunistic infections, women were denied necessary treatment, disability benefits, education, and counseling.

Clearly, the definition could not be changed every time a new opportunistic infection was identified. It needed to be broad enough to include the new cases. What could be standardized, however, was that as a person's CD4 count went down, the disease progressed. With a CD4 count of $1000/mm^3$ considered normal, a person was defined as having AIDS when the count dropped to $200/mm^3$ or having had any condition on the approved list of opportunistic infections. This simplified diagnosis and reporting and included more individuals that should be defined as having AIDS. People do, however, become ill with CD4 counts above 200. Because of this, it might be better to think of the disease as "HIV spectrum" disease.

Disease Progression with the
CD4 Count Model

The progression of HIV infection can be tracked with CD4 counts. The timing varies from patient to patient but does follow a general pattern.

Three Stages

In the early stage of HIV infection, the CD4 count is normal (between 800 and $1500/mm^3$). This stage begins with HIV entering the body. It cannot usually be detected for up to 10 weeks and sometimes longer. During this time, flulike symptoms appear and then disappear. Most people remain asymptomatic for a long time. This stage lasts an average of five years but varies greatly.

By the start of the middle stage, the CD4 count has dropped to $500/mm^3$. Many people are still asymptomatic at this point. Treatment with *AZT* and other antiviral drugs is recommended (see chapter 7). Tests will show that the body's immune system is starting to deteriorate. This stage lasts about five years.

The late stage of HIV infection is reached when the CD4 count reaches $200/mm^3$. Some patients are still asymptomatic. The risk of infection from bacteria, fungi, viruses, parasites, and cancer is very high. Many experience diarrhea, weight loss, tiredness, and fevers. A fungal infection known as thrush (white coating and spots on the tongue and mouth) is common. The immune system rapidly fails, allowing for opportunistic infections to take over. This stage lasts on average three years.

Viral Load

The amount of virus present in the blood is known as viral load. From the moment of infection, HIV reproduces quickly and continuously. This produces an enormous strain on the immune system, which tries to keep up.

About two billion new viruses are produced each day. The body tries to keep up and produces about two billion new CD4 cells each day. In most patients, the immune system cannot keep up. Eventually more viruses than CD4 cells are produced, and CD4 cells are destroyed by the HIV disease process.

As a result, viral load increases, CD4 counts go down, and AIDS symptoms begin to develop. Viral load is a good indicator of disease progress. Recent research has shown that people with high viral loads early in the disease developed AIDS much faster than those with early low levels of the virus. In addition, it has been shown that reduction in viral load slows the progression of the disease.

Viral loads and CD4 counts are used together to measure disease progress. As the disease progresses, CD4 counts drop. The speed at which this progress is taking place is measured by viral load. Low viral load indicates slow disease progress. High viral load suggests fast disease progress. (See chapter 6, Viral Load Testing.)

Pediatric HIV Infection

Most cases of pediatric HIV (HIV in children) were contracted from an infected mother. This might have happened either before or during birth or from being breast-fed. Transmission in children has also occurred from blood transfusions, organ or tissue transplants, sexual contact, and needle contamination. Many cases were documented in the former Soviet Union, where nonsterile needles were used in treating pediatric patients.

Diagnosis
Positive diagnosis is difficult with pediatric cases. Children born to HIV positive mothers carry their mother's antibodies until about 18 months of age. After 18 months, a positive

An infant with AIDS stands in his crib. In most cases of pediatric HIV, the virus is transferred from mother to child.

HIV antibody test shows actual infection. We can know this at four weeks with a PCR (*polymerase chain reaction*) test, which detects viral DNA. (See chapter 6.)

Symptoms

Clinical symptoms may be present at an early age, sometime before age six months. Early indicators may include anemia, cardiac abnormalities, chronic and recurring diarrhea, growth retardation, enlarged liver, herpes zoster, intestinal abnormalities, lymphadenopathy, lymphocytic interstitial pneumonia (LIP), middle ear infections, mucous membrane lesions, neurocognitive defects, oral candidiasis, *Pneumocystis carinii* pneumonia (PCP), parotid gland enlargement, persistent fever of unknown origin, recurring viral or bacterial infections, regression through developmental milestones, salmonella infection, enlarged spleen, and wasting syndrome.

Many of these opportunistic infections are similar to those in adults. More than 90 percent of the HIV-infected children have cardiac abnormalities. Many have coinfection with other viruses, most common of which is cytomegalovirus (CMV). CMV has been found in 65 percent of HIV-positive children. Gastrointestinal complications are found in most infected children, especially diarrhea and impaired intestinal function.

Pattern of Infection

Two patterns of HIV disease progression have been identified in pediatric cases. The exact reason for this is still being researched. Infants who show symptoms before age one often develop an acute, rapidly progressing form of AIDS. Death occurs on average within 7 to 12 months of diagnosis. Children who become symptomatic after age two usually develop a chronic, more prolonged form of the disease. Some children born with HIV infection have remained asymptomatic. They enjoy healthy childhoods.

Developmental Disabilities

Children born with HIV infection show many developmental (learning) disabilities. They often need special tutoring in school. This is because HIV affects the brain and learning function. HIV destroys brain cells, which shows up as dementia in adults.

Many children born to HIV-positive mothers do *not* themselves have HIV infection. Unfortunately, many still show developmental disabilities. When they reach school age, they may have learning problems. The exact reason is still being researched. Speculation is that, similar to fetal alcohol syndrome (a disease that affects children in mothers who drink heavily while pregnant), the mother's disease condition is affecting the infant during prenatal growth.

Opportunistic Infections

Although many advances have been made in HIV treatment in the last few years, opportunistic infections still cause most of the hospitalizations, disabilities, and death. Most of these diseases would not appear if the immune system was working properly. Let's review some of the more common opportunistic infections.

Candidiasis (Thrush)

Candidiasis is caused by *Candida*, a fungus similar to baker's yeast. It is found on the skin and mucosal surfaces. White furry patches form in the mouth. It can spread to the esophagus, causing pain during swallowing. About 50 percent of HIV-infected patients will experience candidiasis, which is also known as thrush.

Histoplasmosis

Histoplasmosis is a fungal disease caused by an organism found in the soil and often spread by bird droppings. It infects the lungs and blood and can continue to grow and spread throughout the body. It causes fever, weight loss, breathing problems, lesions, and anemia.

Shingles

Shingles, also known as herpes zoster, is a painful rash caused by *Varicella zoster*, the same virus that causes chicken pox. It is a member of the *herpes virus* family. After childhood chicken pox, the virus remains dormant for many years. When the immune system is weakened, shingles appear. Non-AIDS patients can also suffer from shingles, but not as severely.

Hairy Leukoplakia

Hairy leukoplakia is an abnormal condition in which plaque appears in the mouth. The plaque is an unusual growth of papillae cells of the tongue. The cells cannot be scraped off. The growth resembles cancer, but it's a result of infection with *Epstein-Barr virus*, also a member of the herpes virus family. Epstein-Barr causes infectious mononucleosis in young adults, but hairy leukoplakia is a condition unique to AIDS patients.

Cytomegalovirus (CMV)

Cytomegalovirus (CMV) is a common virus that infects many people. A member of the herpes virus family, it tends to infect the eyes and cause blindness. It can also produce a form of pneumonia and other symptoms, including rashes, fever, and gastroenteritis. People with normal immune system function can keep it in check.

Pneumocystis Carinii Pneumonia (PCP)

Pneumocystis carinii pneumonia (PCP) is a form of pneumonia that is the most serious opportunistic infection in AIDS patients. It infects about half of all patients and is the leading cause of death. Patients have a dry cough and shortness of breath. This disease is caused by *Pneumocystis carinii*, a protozoan found in water and soil.

Cryptosporidiosis
Cryptosporidiosis is an intestinal disease caused by the *cryptosporidium* protozoan. It causes diarrhea, which occurs 20 to 50 times per day, with cramps, weight loss, and serious loss of body fluid.

Toxoplasmosis
Toxoplasmosis is a serious protozoan disease caused by the protozoan *Toxoplasma gondii*. It is found in raw or undercooked meat and in cat feces. This organism invades many body organs. In AIDS patients, the brain is often infected, causing convulsions, disorientation, and dementia.

Tuberculosis
AIDS patients are highly susceptible to tuberculosis (TB) and can be infected with several forms of the bacteria. The most common TB infection is caused by *Mycobacterium avium-intracellulaire*. This bacteria does not normally cause disease in healthy people. It infects not only the lungs but also other tissues, such as bone marrow. Strains of the bacteria have become resistant to the drugs that have been used to treat TB. Many of these strains are infecting AIDS patients, and they in turn are transmitting it to others.

Mycobacteria Avium Complex
Mycobacteria avium complex (MAC or MAI) is caused by the bacteria *Mycobacterium avium*, which is found in water, soil, dust, and food. The bacteria infects such organs as lungs, intestines, liver, and lymph nodes. It causes fever, diarrhea,

weight loss, stomach pains, fatigue, enlarged liver and spleen, and tissue masses.

Kaposi's Sarcoma
Before the HIV epidemic, Kaposi's sarcoma was seen only in older men of Mediterranean or Jewish ancestry. In homosexual men with AIDS, the disease appears in about 70 percent of the patients. Kaposi's sarcoma is a tumor of the blood vessels. It appears as pink, purple, or brown skin lesions, usually on the arms and legs, and eventually spreads to linings of the body.

Cervical Cancer
Cancer of the cervix is common among female AIDS patients. The human papilloma virus (HPV) that also causes *genital warts* is thought to cause some cervical cancer. Infection with HPV usually occurs from sexual contact. Cervical cancer can also be caused by other factors, such as smoking.

Lymphoma
Lymphomas are cancers of the B cells of the immune system. These cells become infected with Epstein-Barr virus, which may be important in the development of lymphomas. AIDS patients get an unusual form of lymphoma that spreads to the brain.

AIDS Dementia
HIV infection can cause damage to brain cells, which leads to a loss of mental function known as dementia. This process happens slowly and may first appear as simple forgetfulness and then progress to difficulty in reasoning and performing mental tasks. Depression and personality changes are common.

CHAPTER 5

TRANSMISSION
AND SPREAD
OF HIV

HIV INFECTION IS SPREAD THROUGH THE EXCHANGE OF infected blood, *semen*, vaginal fluid, and breast milk. Other fluids, such as cerebral spinal fluid, can also transmit the virus. But the average person does not come in contact with cerebral spinal fluid.

HIV is a blood-borne *pathogen* (something that causes disease), which means it needs blood to survive. HIV dies quickly on contact with air.[1] The body fluids that can carry the virus all have blood in them. More specifically, they have white blood cells (CD4 cells) in them. Vaginal fluid may contain white blood cells from vaginal infections. White blood cells are the cells that become infected with HIV, so the more white blood cells in the fluid, the more risky the fluid is for transmission. These fluids can be placed in risk order based on the amount of white blood cells they contain. From most risky to least risky, the order is blood, semen, vaginal fluid, and breast milk.

Intact skin is an excellent barrier to HIV infection. HIV-infected blood, however, does have the potential of getting into an open cut or sore of another person. This has rarely occurred, but the potential is there. For this reason, it is important to always follow universal precautions.

Other body fluids that do not have blood in them do *not* spread HIV. You cannot get HIV from tears, sweat, urine, feces, saliva, mucus, vomit, or earwax. Some of these fluids may carry other diseases, but not HIV. If, however, these fluids do have visible blood in them, they can be infectious from unkilled HIV or other diseases.

The Centers for Disease Control and Prevention (CDC) have established a simple rule for urine, vomit, or other fluids: If you can see blood (red) in it, treat it as if it were blood, and infected. If you cannot see red, the amount of blood is too small to be of real concern for HIV. But remember, you can get other diseases from these fluids. Therefore always follow universal precautions. Use gloves for cleaning of blood, urine, or feces and disinfect floors or furniture with a 1 to 10 solution of bleach (or Lysol spray on fabric that would be stained by bleach). Never put dirty hands in your mouth or eyes. After you take off the gloves, wash your hands with warm water and soap.

How HIV Is Not Spread

You do not catch HIV the way you catch a cold or the flu. HIV is not spread from hugging, kissing, shaking hands, dancing, sharing food, drinking from a fountain, sitting on a toilet seat, or swimming in a pool or hot tub. You cannot get it in a restaurant, even if the waitress or cook is infected. You do not get HIV from someone coughing, sneezing, or spitting on you.

Teen couples like to show affection for each other.
HIV is not spread through such casual contact as hugging
and kissing; it is spread from the exchange of fluids during
sexual intercourse, from an infected mother to her child,
and from the sharing of infected needles.

Touching

You do not get HIV from massage, tickling, or other contact with healthy skin. The skin is an excellent barrier for germs, including HIV. Any exposure to HIV on the skin is destroyed by exposure to air or mild disinfectants, such as soap and warm water, or other mild cleansers.

Kissing

As far as we know, no one has ever gotten HIV from kissing.[2] Theoretically you could get HIV from French-kissing (open-mouth, deep, or tongue kissing) someone who is HIV infected. Here, both people would have to have open sores on their mouth, lips, or gums. Blood from the bleeding infected person would have to get into the mouth sores of the other person.

Regular kissing is not a risk, even if saliva is exchanged. Saliva is a poor transmitter of HIV. It does not contain white blood cells, and it has a natural antibiotic substance that kills HIV. Any HIV found in saliva is few in number and short lived. Researchers agree that kissing poses a very small risk.

Scientists from the National Institute of Dental Research (NIDR) have discovered the protein believed to be responsible for saliva's anti-HIV properties. It is called secretory leukocyte protease inhibitor, or SLPI (pronounced "slippy"). SLPI works by interacting with white blood cells, not HIV. Although researchers aren't sure how, SLPI seems to keep HIV out. They hope this may help them find a way of protecting people exposed to HIV-infected blood.

Giving Blood

You cannot get HIV from giving blood. When you donate blood, a brand new needle is used to take the blood. The needle is destroyed when you are finished giving blood. You are a blood donor, not a blood recipient, so you're not getting blood or any germs from another person. Don't be afraid to give blood. It is an important way to help others.

Mosquitoes

You cannot get HIV from mosquitoes. When you are bitten by a mosquito, you are a blood donor, not a blood recipient. What happens when a mosquito bites you? It lands on your skin and sticks its mouth into your skin. It regurgitates saliva into your skin to keep your blood from coagulating. This is what makes your skin itch after the bite. Then the mosquito sucks blood out. This blood goes into its stomach, where it is digested. When the mosquito is hungry again, the process is repeated. No blood from the first person gets into you. You cannot get HIV from other biting or stinging insects such as fleas, lice, or flies.

How HIV Is Spread

HIV is spread in three ways: from the exchange of infected fluids during *sexual intercourse*, from an infected mother to her child, and from the sharing of infected needles.

Sexual Transmission

The primary way HIV is transmitted throughout the world is through sexual contact. Through June 1996, 59 percent of Americans who were diagnosed with AIDS contracted the disease from having sex with an infected person. Among adolescents and young adults (13–24), through June 1996, 67 percent[3] who were diagnosed with AIDS contracted the disease from having sex with an infected person. An additional 11 percent of the cases had multiple risks, including sex.

There are three types of sexual intercourse: oral, vaginal, and anal. HIV can be transmitted during sexual intercourse if the virus in the blood, semen, or vaginal fluid of the infected person comes in contact with and gets into the body of the other person. Blood includes menstrual blood, blood from cuts or sores, and bleeding from rough sex. Anal sex is particularly dangerous because it can easily cause rectal bleeding. Here, feces might be infected because of the infected blood they contain. Semen, a mixture of sperm and male sexual fluids, is released when a man ejaculates, or comes. A drop of this fluid often comes out of the penis when a man is sexually aroused, or turned on. Even this pre-ejaculatory fluid can contain the virus in an infected male. Vaginal fluid is produced by glands inside the vagina and keeps the tissues moist and lubricated during sex. It can carry HIV in an infected woman.

Transmission takes place when these infected body fluids find an opening in the skin. If white blood cells carrying the virus from these fluids get into those openings, the person becomes infected. Openings do not necessarily mean cuts or tears in the skin. Moist tissue in body openings, like the vaginal canal, the urinary opening at the tip of the penis, the rectum, or even the moist tissue inside the eye or at the back of the throat has microscopic openings for the virus to get in. Actually, the anus, urethra, vaginal canal, and back of the throat have columnar epithelial tissue, to which the virus binds. This is why mucous membranes are considered a problem for transmission. When there are open sores or rashes on the penis or vagina, finding an entrance into the body is even easier for the virus.

For these reasons, all forms of sexual intercourse with an infected partner can place a person at risk for HIV infection. The risks, however, are not equal. We can rank order the risk. From high to low they are anal, vaginal, then oral intercourse.

Anal intercourse is the riskiest form of intercourse. It involves the male placing his penis in the rectum of his partner. Anal sex is practiced by both heterosexual (opposite sex) and homosexual (same sex) couples. Anal intercourse is risky for two reasons. First, the rectum was not designed for sexual intercourse. It does not stretch like the vaginal canal. It is, therefore, susceptible to tearing and bleeding. These tears provide a natural opening for the virus to get in. In addition, the large intestine is a nonsterile environment. To prevent this nonsterile environment from infecting the body, the intestine contains a layer of white blood cells to fight off infection. These white blood cells are the very CD4 cells that pick up HIV. These cells then transport the virus into the body. This can happen even if there is no tearing and bleeding during anal intercourse.

Vaginal intercourse with an infected person is a definite risk. This is the most common form of sexual intercourse. The man puts his penis inside the vagina of the woman. Semen coming out of the man's penis or vaginal fluid produced by the woman can carry HIV. Even when there are no irritations or breaks in the vaginal wall, microscopic openings in the mucous membrane and the lining of epithelial cells can allow the virus into the body. The virus can also infect men through the urethra of the penis.

Oral intercourse is the least risky form of intercourse for HIV transmission. Also known as oral-genital sex, it involves using the mouth or tongue to stimulate the other person's sex organs. Both heterosexual and homosexual males and females practice this form of intercourse. The risk of HIV infection is low from oral sex for two reasons. First there is a large amount of saliva in the mouth. The antibiotic action of the saliva helps kill or inactivate HIV before it can get into the body. Second, if infected fluids (semen or vaginal fluid) are swallowed, the strong stomach acid in an adult will kill the virus. It seems that the most vulnerable spots are the columnar epithelial cells of the mucous membrane at the back of the throat or open sores in the gums or mouth. There have not been any well-documented cases of HIV transmission via the mouth, but it is *not* risk free. More research needs to be done in this area.

It is important to remember that both men and women are at risk. During heterosexual sex, the woman is at greater risk. This is because there are more openings in the mucous membrane of the vaginal canal than in the urethra of the penis. What is more important, semen stays in the vaginal canal for many hours providing longer exposure. The vaginal canal and the cervix can then have more time to act as a receptor for HIV. In addition, infected semen usually contains more virus than infected vaginal fluid. During intercourse the semen is deposited in the vaginal canal and remains there long enough to cause infection. Infected vaginal fluid may not stay on the penis very long. After intercourse, when the penis is withdrawn from the vagina, it is exposed to the air that will kill any virus on the outside. HIV can remain active as long as it is moist. When infected vaginal fluid, semen, or blood is *thoroughly* dry, exposed to the air, HIV is no longer active.

Some partners of infected individuals have been infected after having intercourse only once. Others, in spite of repeated exposure, have not become infected. The reason for this is somewhat of a mystery, but we do have some clues. The higher the level of virus (high viral load) in the infected person's blood, the greater the risk of infection. As with other germs, some people are more resistant than others. Research has found that tobacco, alcohol, and other drugs weaken the immune system. Use of these substances seems to make a person more susceptible.

The more often a person has intercourse and the more sexual partners a person has, the greater the chances are of becoming infected. If one partner has another sexually transmitted disease (STD), the chances of HIV transmission go up. Other STDs, such as *gonorrhea* or syphilis, cause sores that provide openings for the virus to get in.

Several studies have shown that uncircumcised men have a higher risk of getting HIV and transmitting it to their

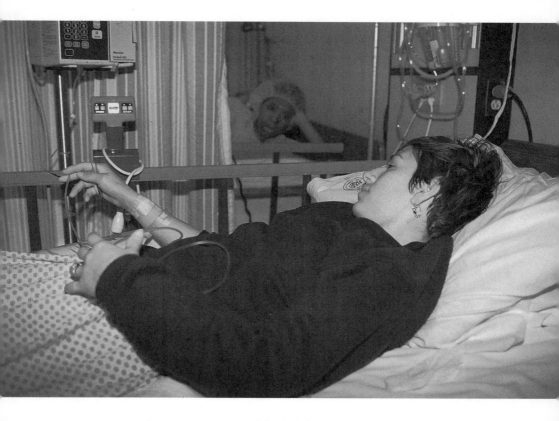

*A young woman with AIDS receives treatment
at a hospital. Women are at greater risk of contracting
HIV during heterosexual sexual contact than men.*

partners. Circumcision is the removal of the foreskin of the penis. The operation is usually done during the first week after a baby boy is born. If the foreskin has not been removed, the chances are greater that dirt, bacteria, viruses, and infection will accumulate under the foreskin. Some men even have small sores under the foreskin that provide openings for the virus to get in or out.

Sexual intercourse during a woman's period may increase the chances of transmission. Increased blood in the vaginal area can make transmission to the male easier. Openings in the vaginal canal from menstrual bleeding leave the woman with more areas for the virus to enter her body.

Studies have shown that women who have HIV-positive partners and use oral contraceptives are less likely to become infected. Oral contraceptives tend to thicken the cervical mucus. This may slow the passage of infected cells in semen once they encounter the cervix. Oral contraceptives, however, are *not* a substitute for the barrier methods of HIV prevention, such as using *condoms*. Use of an intrauterine device (IUD) has been associated with an increased risk of transmission. The IUD may cause inflammation of the uterine mucosa. The inflammation causes white blood cells to pool in that area. These cells are highly susceptible to HIV infection.

Women who have sex with women are at risk of HIV infection. The level of risk depends on their sexual practices. Use of sex toys, sexual activity around the menstrual cycle, and pre-existing STDs influences the risk.

New research has shown that some people—perhaps one in 100 whites—have a mutated gene that might protect them from HIV infection. This may explain why some people have repeated risky sex and still do not become infected. The gene controls CCR5, which normally helps CD4 act as a docking station for HIV. When the gene is defective, the docking between CD4 and HIV is slowed or prevented. Some people have one defective gene (getting it from one parent) and some have two (getting them from both parents). The effects of having only one is still unclear, but researchers believe it may make people less likely to be infected. People with two of these genes seem to get no infection. How long this protection will last is still unknown. As this research continues, it may open possibilities for treatment and prevention.

Mother-to-Child Transmission

As of July 1996, 90 percent of the pediatric cases of AIDS in the United States were diagnosed in babies born to HIV-positive mothers. The remainder were infected by other means, such as infected needles, child abuse, or infected blood products. The World Health Organization (WHO) estimates that 5 percent to 10 percent of the current global total HIV infections were transmitted from mother to infant during pregnancy, or about 1.5 million children. These transmissions seem to occur in about 25 percent of completed pregnancies in HIV-infected women.

Several studies have tried to learn or predict what pregnancy risk factors might influence transmission. Whether the mother seroconverted before or during pregnancy; birth order of twins; proximity of a lower-lying twin to the cervix; fetal position; and natural vs. cesarean birth are risk factors that have been considered. No definite conclusions have resulted from the research.

HIV has been detected in breast milk of HIV-infected women. Transmission after birth has been documented in breast-fed babies of infected mothers. There is much disagreement, however, whether transmission occurs from the milk. Some research has shown that the HIV level is higher in colostrum, the milky substance secreted from the breast before and just after birth, than in breast milk. The frequency of transmission is also under question. There is also a question of whether transmission is more likely from mothers infected before delivery as opposed to those infected after delivery.

A mathematically predictive breast-feeding study was done using the numbers of infected mothers in New York City. It predicted that if all HIV-infected mothers did not breast-feed their infants, 5 fewer babies would die, but 58 more infants would die if all the uninfected mothers did not breast-feed. This is because breast-feeding helps prevent infection and disease in children. Because of this uncertainty, many countries still encourage women to breast feed.

Transmission in Drug Users

Worldwide, injecting drug use is the second largest cause of HIV transmission. In the United States, in 1995, it was responsible for 85 percent of the cases among heterosexual men.[4] Sixty-six percent of the cases among women in 1995 were transmitted either by sharing needles or through sexual contact with a drug user. Sharing needles is a high-risk activity for blood-to-blood transmission. The risk of transmission increases with the frequency of injection, frequency of using shared needles, and injecting in shooting galleries (places people go to shoot drugs and where needles are often shared).

Drug users, especially crack users, tend to also be sexually active. A crack high often produces an enhanced sexual drive, and sex is a common way to get money to buy drugs. Therefore, crack users and other drug users—even those who do not inject needles—are at greater risk of HIV. In addition, drug and alcohol use tends to impair judgment. This puts them at greater risk of contracting HIV from sex or just wanting to try a new drug. People can also black out from alcohol or drug use, meaning that they do not remember what they did and with whom. They have no memory of their risks. For all these reasons, having sex with a person who has used drugs, especially needles, can be very risky.

Needle sharing for any reason is dangerous. If a diabetic shared needles to take insulin, this is risky. Athletes who share needles when taking steroids are at risk of HIV. *Never share needles for any reason.*

The injected drug does not spread HIV, it is the sharing of the needles or *works*—syringes, eye droppers, needles, spoons or other items used to prepare the drug—that does. When a person injects or shoots drugs, blood is drawn back

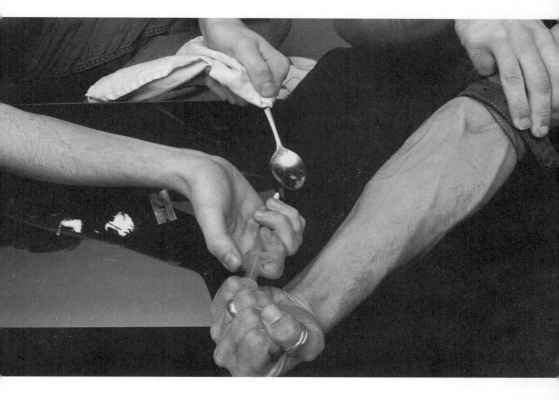

A young man prepares to inject heroin into a friend's vein. Sharing needles is a high-risk factor for contracting HIV.

into the needle and syringe. Some blood from the first person may remain in the needle. If the person is HIV-infected, the virus will be in the blood. The next person or persons who use the equipment can get HIV. Old needles that have not been used for a long time may still be infected because HIV can survive a long time inside needles. This is because blood remains in the hollow of the needle, where there is often no air.

Once people start using drugs, they can become *addicted*. This is especially true for injection drugs. Because you need a prescription in some states, needles are often expensive or hard to get. In some states and countries, needles are legal to possess without a prescription. Where they are available for purchase at pharmacies, there is a significantly lower rate of HIV infection among needle users, women, and children.

Some places have needle exchange programs, where addicts can bring in old needles and exchange them for new ones.[5] Addicts may start to feel sick if they go too long without the drug. When they finally get the drug, they often need a fix so badly that they do not take the time to sterilize the needle. They also may not have anything to sterilize it with.

Drug users may not think clearly. Needle users often believe that only someone else will get HIV. They may not bother cleaning the needles or works. Users often shoot up with friends. It is a group activity. For some, cleaning needles is an insult. It implies that the friend is not clean or is infected.

Many drug users go to shooting galleries to get drugs. These are often in abandoned buildings or unclean locations. Equipment or supplies for sterilizing works are often not available there. At shooting galleries, people often rent out or share works. They may be used by many people each day. The HIV infection rate is very high among those who frequent shooting galleries.

A common practice in many cities is for addicts to sell repackaged needles. These are sold as clean needles but are really not clean. Addicts are selling their old needles to make money to buy more drugs. Never trust a needle bought on the street.

CHAPTER 6

HIV
TESTING

DURING THE PAST DECADE, SIGNIFICANT ADVANCES HAVE been made in HIV testing. This has been important for disease control, safety of the blood supply, and information on the spread of HIV infection. Routine testing of all donated blood for the presence of HIV started in 1985 in most industrialized nations. Since then, testing methods have become more sensitive, more specific, and faster. Tests are now available to identify HIV-1 and HIV-2 and their cousins, HTLV-I and HTLV-II. Depending on the geographic area, one or all these tests are used. The newest type of HIV testing is the home testing kit. With the development of new tests, there is greater hope for early detection.

Testing Methods

Three basic types of tests are available: indirect signaling of HIV presence by the detection of antibodies, direct detection of the virus or its parts, or viral load testing.

Indirect Methods

Most testing for HIV is done by indirect methods. These tests detect products of the immune response by finding the presence of HIV antibodies. They are very sensitive but work only when the HIV antibody level reaches a critical level for the test.

A significant problem with HIV antibody testing is the *seroconversion window*. Seroconversion is the time when the body has enough antibodies in response to an antigen invasion needed for test detection. There is a lag time between infection and when antibody levels reach a critical mass level for detection. This is called the seroconversion window period. For HIV infection, the window generally lasts three to six months after infection. These differences in time are usually due to a person's ability to produce antibodies. This ability varies from person to person.

For large-scale screening of blood, the *ELISA* and *Western blot* are still the most reliable and cost-effective tests. The two tests are done in conjunction with each other. ELISA is designed to be oversensitive. It is a mass screening tool. ELISA catches even questionable blood samples. It has also been known to show positive with other conditions, including diabetes and some liver conditions. Therefore, some positive ELISA results are false positive (See p. 75, "False Positive and False Negative Results"). When labs get a positive ELISA, they retest with another ELISA. If the results are still positive, they then do a different test. This confirmation test is usually a Western blot test. Using other confirmation tests—such as immunofluorescence *assay*, radioimmunoprecipitation assay, or even direct-testing methods—is possible.

ELISA tests use HIV antigens, which react to antibodies in the patient's blood sample. A chemical is then added to the mixture. If the antibody-antigen reaction is present, the mixture will change color. The color change shows a

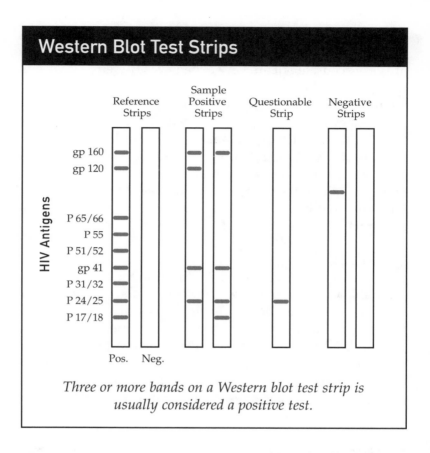

Western Blot Test Strips

HIV Antigens

Reference Strips   Sample Positive Strips   Questionable Strip   Negative Strips

gp 160
gp 120
P 65/66
P 55
P 51/52
gp 41
P 31/32
P 24/25
P 17/18

Pos.   Neg.

Three or more bands on a Western blot test strip is usually considered a positive test.

positive test. Most of the new home test kits are this type of test.

Western blot tests detect specific antibodies in a patient's blood. The test works by separating HIV proteins by weight. The proteins are then absorbed onto special paper strips. If antibodies are present in the blood sample, they show up as bands on the paper strips. The bands represent specific antibodies. So the test is not an all-or-nothing test like ELISA. It is positive or negative for specific antibodies of HIV.

Direct Methods

Direct diagnostic tests identify the virus itself. These tests are very accurate but are very expensive. Therefore, they are not good for large-scale screening. Some techniques used include virus isolation by culture techniques.

The newest direct method is the polymerase chain reaction (PCR) test. This gene amplification technique detects DNA produced by HIV in the viral replication. This is the only test that theoretically can provide positive evidence of HIV throughout the course of the disease. Because the virus has times of low reproductive activity, other tests may not detect its presence when in fact it is there.

Viral Load Testing

Viral load tests show how much virus is in the blood. Results of viral load tests can range from almost none to more than a million. Low numbers mean less virus in the blood and therefore less active disease. High numbers mean more virus in the blood and more active disease. Viral load tests are often given for several reasons. They may be taken to get a baseline viral count, to see if antiviral medications are working, or to decide if a change in medication is needed.

Meaning of Viral Load Test Results

VIRAL LOAD TEST	CHANCES for a WORSENING of the DISEASE
$10,000/mm^3$ or less	Low risk
$10,000$ to $100,000/mm^3$	Medium risk
$100,000/mm^3$ or more	High risk

False Positive and False Negative Results

An important aspect of any testing is getting correct results. There is always the possibility of incorrect results: a false positive or false negative.

A false positive occurs when the test shows that a person has the disease, but the person is really disease free. False positives do not pose any disease threat. They do, however, create unnecessary anxiety on the part of patients, their partners, and their family. It is estimated that about 1 out of every 100,000 HIV antibody tests results in a false positive.

A false negative occurs when the test shows the person has no infection, but the person is really infected. False negatives usually occur when the amount of antibodies or virus is lower than the level needed to trigger the test as positive. The person is usually in the window period. False negatives pose a serious threat to health. They can result in contaminated blood getting into the blood bank system or infected donor body parts being used. They can also contribute to an unsuspecting partner getting the virus. False negatives are one important reason for HIV counseling always to accompany testing. It allows the person to interpret the results and decide what next steps to take, such as repeat testing.

Testing Children Born to HIV Positive Mothers

During fetal development, any antibody a mother has produced will cross the placenta and enter the fetus. This is true of antibodies for any disease, including HIV. This gives newborn babies disease protection in early life before they can produce their own antibodies. It is a protective mechanism.

In addition, infected mothers who breast-feed may transfer HIV and HIV antibodies through breast milk.

Cracked, bleeding nipples may also be a source of HIV to the nursing child.

These two factors make HIV disease detection in newborns and children of HIV positive mothers very difficult. Are the detected antibodies from the mother or from the child? Antibody tests cannot be used on newborns until at least 18 months of age and sometimes longer. After this time, babies lose their mother's HIV antibodies and will produce their own, if they are infected.

Therefore, in early testing of newborns, PCR tests, which detect the actual virus, produce the best results and are accurate for infants more than one month old. This is an area of research that may produce new methods and knowledge in the next few years.

Voluntary vs. Mandatory Testing

One of the most controversial issues played out in the AIDS arena is determining who should be tested. Should HIV tests be mandatory or voluntary? Some suggest mandatory testing would change "undesirable" behavior, such as promiscuous sex, drug use, and homosexuality. Others feel that testing and public knowledge of a person's HIV status would jeopardize jobs, housing, insurance, and education. From the behavior of much of the public toward HIV-infected individuals, the latter is clearly true. Until the public is more educated, mandatory testing probably will not work.

Because of the window period, and because people are often not willing partners in mandated testing, a false sense of security can occur. Some negative test results would produce the reaction, "See, I told you I didn't have AIDS!" In fact, the person may be incubating and spreading a deadly virus. When the test is voluntary, the person is there because they know there may be a problem.

As a result, many states have passed laws requiring that testing only be done voluntarily on informed individuals with their specific consent. The few exceptions to this are testing to get into the military, to get insurance, and testing of newborns for research purposes and epidemic tracking.

The issue of mandatory testing for pregnant women has become increasingly controversial as the rate of HIV infection continues to rise. An estimated 65,000 HIV-positive women gave birth in 1993. Early detection and AZT (see chapter 7) could reduce the number of children born with HIV. New York State has required testing of all pregnant women with notification of results. Other states are expected to follow this procedure in the future.

Testing is most effective when accompanied by pre- and posttest counseling, so many states mandate counseling. The counselor must fully explain the benefits and risks of testing. Following the testing, counselors explain the significance of the results. If the test is positive, the counselor helps deal with the impact of the reality and finds further counseling and treatment for the person.

Confidential vs. Anonymous Testing

In many places, two testing and information receiving procedures are in effect: confidential testing and anonymous testing. With confidential testing, the test site knows your identity. With anonymous testing, you are only a number; they do not know your name. With either method, there is counseling, and you must be there in person to get the results.

CHAPTER 7

IN SEARCH
OF A CURE

UNFORTUNATELY THERE IS NO CURE OR VACCINE FOR HIV infection or AIDS, its final stage. Scientists have been working for more than a decade on this problem, but no "magic bullet" has been found. The virus does not respond to standard treatments used with other diseases.

A major scientific goal has been to slow or stop the virus. Although we are not there yet, some progress has been made. There are two major groups of medications taken by HIV patients: *antivirals* and treatments for specific opportunistic infections. Research in the field of medications is going on at an intense rate. Many drug companies are researching new products, and researchers expect that great advances will take place in the next few years.

Antiviral Medications

HIV is a retrovirus. After HIV enters the body, it infects and takes control of CD4 cells. When the virus infects the cell, it combines its genetic material with that of the cell. The cell and the virus become bound together as one unit. The cell then becomes a factory for producing more HIV. *Reverse transcriptase* allows the virus to change its RNA into viral DNA that can be used by the host cell. There are different types of antiviral drugs, which work by interfering in different ways with the process of infecting cells and reproducing more HIV.

The most common antiviral drugs for HIV are reverse transcriptase inhibitors. Some of these are nucleoside analogs, which look very much like the viruses' genetic material but are different enough to interfere with viral replication. They do this by using "defective building blocks." The virus uses these blocks by mistake to make copies of itself. By using these incorrect parts, the virus's replication process stops.

These drugs are very strong medications, and their side effects may make them difficult for some people to take. Reverse transcriptase inhibitors do not eliminate the virus from the body, and so they do not cure the infection. In addition, because the virus can change itself so easily, it can produce a new strain that is no longer affected by these drugs.

A newer class of drugs called protease inhibitors also interferes with the replication process. They work at the final stage of viral assembly. This takes place after the virus is inside the CD4 cell and is ready to begin production of new viruses. It prevents new viruses from assembling inside infected cells.

Today, the most successful drug therapy plans combine medications in a multi-drug approach. When protease inhibitors are taken with nucleoside analogs, CD4 counts rise, and viral load drops. No one knows how long the drugs will work. It is hoped that the drugs may eventually be able to eradicate the virus from the body.

Treatment for Anti-Viral Drug Therapy

Targets for Antiviral Drug Therapy in the Life Cycle of HIV

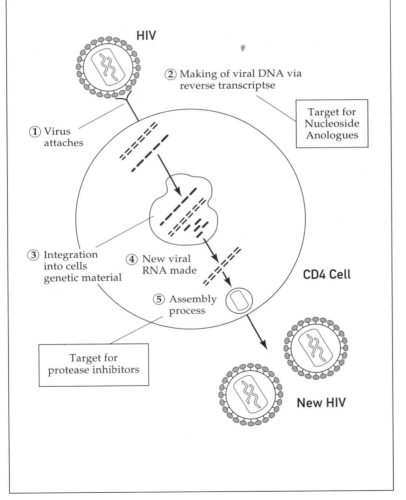

AZT

AZT, also called zidovudine or Retrovir®, is the oldest and most widely used HIV nucleoside antiviral drug. When used alone, it increases patient survival time and reduces the number and severity of opportunistic infections. Because of viral *mutations*, its effect diminishes between 6 and 12 months after use begins. AZT therapy seems to work best when it is taken after the CD4 count drops below $500/mm^3$. The positive effects of AZT are compounded when it is taken in combination with other antivirals. The side effects of AZT include headaches, nausea, high blood pressure, anemia (low level of oxygen in the blood), and low white blood cell counts.

There are major benefits of AZT. Of all the antivirals, AZT seems to have the greatest ability to reduce dementia. This is attributed to its high ability to cross the blood-brain barrier. Special cells surround blood vessels in the brain and spinal cord. These cells prevent some substances in the blood from getting into the cerebrospinal fluid. This is known as blood-brain barrier.

The most profound effect of AZT is its ability to reduce the rate of mother-to-child HIV transmission during pregnancy. Studies have shown that giving HIV-infected pregnant women AZT during pregnancy and delivery and treating newborns for six weeks, resulted in a 66 percent reduction in the number of babies with HIV infection.

ddI

ddI, also called didanosine or Videx®, is a nucleoside analog antiviral. It works the same way as AZT but is less toxic. It can, therefore, be more easily tolerated and provide a good alternative to AZT. ddI is sometimes taken with AZT, and it's common for patients to use AZT for 16 weeks and then switch to ddI. The side effects of ddI include headaches, diarrhea, insomnia, nerve damage to the hands and feet, and increased uric acid levels. (Uric acid is a chemical normally present in the blood. Excessive amounts can result in gout, producing pain and joint destruction.) ddI cannot be absorbed in the stomach's acidic environment, so it must be taken on an empty stomach with a buffer to cut the acid.

ddC

ddC, also called zalcitabine or Hivid®, is a nucleoside analog antiviral. It works in a similar way to AZT and is used as a less toxic alternative to AZT and ddI. Best results with ddC are achieved in people with CD4 counts above 150/mm³ but less than 300/mm³. Side effects of ddC include rashes, chest pain, fever, nausea, elevated liver enzymes, and mouth soreness. These symptoms usually disappear after about two weeks of use. The biggest problem with ddC is getting the dosage correct, which is critical for proper effect.

d4T

d4T, also called stavidine or Zerit®, is a nucleoside analog antiviral. d4T is being used with people who have been on AZT for at least 24 weeks. The switch to d4T improves CD4 cell levels, reduces viral levels, causes weight gain, and causes improved general health. Although the drug is approved, research on it is still under way. Side effects include peripheral nerve damage, increased liver enzymes, and joint and muscle pain.

3TC

3TC, also called lamivudine Epivir®, is the newest nucleoside analog antiviral. Taken with AZT, these two drugs together show a longer sustained reduction of HIV and a longer period of increased CD4 counts. When taken with AZT, the antiviral action seems to start working faster than with AZT alone. Used by itself, 3TC is not effective.

Indinivar

Indinivar, or Crixivan®, is a protease inhibitor. Other brands of protease inhibitors are saquinavir (Invirase®), ritonavir (Norvir®), and nelfinavir (Viracept®). As with nucleoside analogs, HIV develops resistance to these protease inhibitors. If a person develops resistance to one of them, they will probably have developed resistance to all of them. Resistance may be reduced when protease inhibitors are taken with a nucleoside analog and when only one protease inhibitor is taken. Side effects include abdominal pain, nausea, headache, fatigue, insomnia, and constipation. Each of these protease inhibitors has different instructions for use, including time of day to be taken and whether to do so with or without food. With these medications, it is very critical for directions to be followed exactly.

Opportunistic Infection Medications

Drugs used to prevent or delay opportunistic infections for opportunistic infections are prescribed for use at different times. They are used for prophylaxis, or prevention, and treatment. They can also be used to prevent a second or repeated infection. Sometimes these prophylaxis medications are the same as treatment medications, in a lower dose. Other times, they are different drugs altogether.

For most opportunistic infections, there is more than one choice of medication. The doctor and the patient decide together, depending on side effects being experienced and what other medications are being taken. Some medications cannot be used if certain other ones are being taken. Finding the right medication for each person can be a complicated process, which involves trial and error.

The chart on page 84 provides a sampling of medication used to treat opportunistic infections.

Opportunistic Infection	Medication
Mycobacterium Avium Complex	Clarithromycin, Azithromycin
Tuberculosis	Isoniazid, Pyrazinamide, Rifampin
Candidiasis	Fluconazole, Nystatin, Clotrimazole
Cryptococcosis	Fluconazole, Amphotericin-B
Histoplasmosis	Itraconazole, Amphotericin-B, Fluconazole
Cryptosporidiosis	Azithromycin, Paromomycin, Atovaquone
Pneumocystis Carinii Pneumonia	Pemamidine, Co-trimoxazole
Toxoplasmosis	Pyrimethamine and Sulfadiazine or Clindamycin
Cytomegalovirus	Ganciclovir, Foscarnet
Shingles	Acyclovir, Foscarnet, Trifiuridin

Alternative Therapies

The diagnosis of HIV positive is not easy to live with. Suddenly one's life is consumed with doctors, medications, tests, and fears. Despite all the treatments that the medical community can provide, much of the success of treatment and patient longevity lies within each person. Much can be done to stay healthy and improve immune performance. The more actively a person participates in this process, the more fulfilling the rest of his or her life will be.

Nutrition

Nutrition plays an important role in optimal health and functioning of the immune system. Good nutrition provides the energy to get through the day. High sugar and high fat foods hinder immune function. What one eats and when one eats can determine the effectiveness of the medications taken. Some foods, for example, prevent the absorption of medications.

Nutritional intake affects many symptoms of HIV, such as fatigue, diarrhea, fever, nausea, vomiting, painful swallowing, and wasting. Registered dietitians and nutritionists can be helpful in designing appropriate diet modifications for these conditions. They can also help suggest vitamins and supplements to improve nutritional intake.

Acupuncture

Acupuncture is an ancient Chinese method for relieving pain. Short, slender needles are used to pierce the skin at the point of various nerve endings. Each spot corresponds to a particular part of the body, which is relieved of pain and discomfort as a result of this process.

Stress Management

Many stress management techniques provide a feeling of well-being, help one relax, and allow the body to use energy and resources for healing. Progressive relaxation (a method of tensing and loosening muscles to relieve stress), deep breathing, and meditation are helpful. Therapeutic massage improves circulation, promotes healing, and induces a state of deep relaxation. Reflexology, another type of massage,

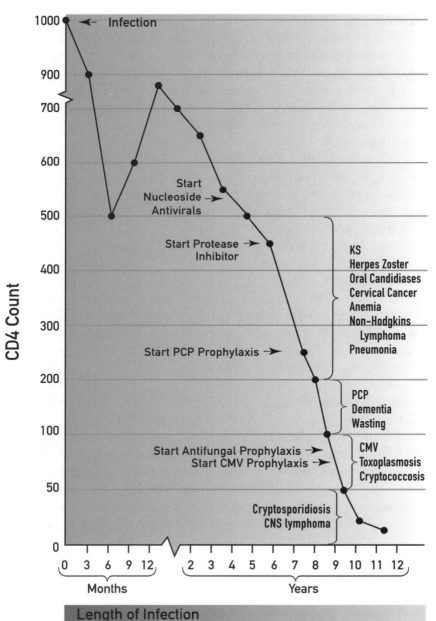

Course of HIV Infection in Adults

Approximate CD4 Markers for Opportunistic
Infections and Treatment

CD4 Count

1000 — ← Infection
900
700
600
Start Nucleoside Antivirals →
500
Start Protease Inhibitor →
400
300
Start PCP Prophylaxis →
200
100
Start Antifungal Prophylaxis →
Start CMV Prophylaxis →
50
Cryptosporidiosis
CNS lymphoma
0

0 3 6 9 12 | 2 3 4 5 6 7 8 9 10 11 12

Months   Years

KS
Herpes Zoster
Oral Candidiases
Cervical Cancer
Anemia
Non-Hodgkins
Lymphoma
Pneumonia

PCP
Dementia
Wasting

CMV
Toxoplasmosis
Cryptococcosis

Length of Infection

involves pressure points on the feet that correspond to different organs and glands of the body. With acupressure, firm pressure is applied to acupoints on the body. These are the same spots used in acupuncture. It enhances the body's natural healing ability and encourages a state of relaxation.

Guided Imagery
With guided imagery, the person focuses on calming mental images to reduce stress. The immune system is improved and the heart rate slows. Guided imagery can be done using audiotapes, group sessions, or one person with a leader.

Hypnosis
Hypnosis is a deeply relaxed state similar to meditation and is used to reduce stress and anxiety, control pain, increase relaxation, and encourage a sense of well-being.

Exercise
Exercise builds muscle and improves cardiovascular fitness and body functioning. Walking, using a treadmill or exercise bike, and weight lifting can be helpful. Working with an exercise physiologist helps ensure that the exercise program is safe and effective. Keeping track of the amount of exercise and checking target heart rates helps ensure progress.

Therapeutic Touch
Based on the idea that an energy field surrounds the body, therapeutic touch rarely involves physical contact. When ill, this energy field is blocked. A specially trained practitioner unblocks the energy by passing the hands a few inches above the body to smooth out the blockage. The therapy increases relaxation and decreases anxiety.

Aroma Therapy

Based on the idea that the smell of certain oils can bring on an emotional response, aroma therapy causes a state of well being.

Helping Others

A positive attitude is most important in dealing with HIV. Helping others is satisfying and gives purpose to life. After coming to terms with their own diagnosis, many HIV-infected people help others cope and talk to groups about their condition and AIDS-related issues. The positive feelings of being helpful and productive can be very fulfilling.

Vaccine Development

The purpose of a vaccine is to evoke an immune system response that will prevent infection or disease development. Vaccines can be given to unexposed people to prevent infection. These are known as preexposure vaccines. Vaccines can also be given to exposed people. These postexposure vaccines eliminate or control infection.

The work of trying to find a vaccine to protect against HIV has been underway for many years. By the end of 1996, more than 20 proposed vaccines got as far as field trials, but the trials all stopped when it was found that the vaccines were not working. It is a tough problem that may someday be solved.

In the past, several types of vaccines have been used against viral diseases. These have included live virus, weakened (*attenuated*) virus, and killed (inactivated) virus. With HIV, however, these methods have considerable risk. Scientists must be sure the ingredients in the vaccine cannot produce HIV infection.

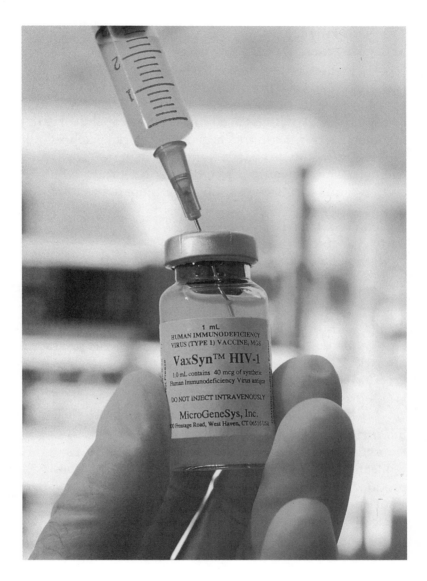

Vaxsyn, an AIDS vaccine, is being used
in clinical trials.

Live and Weakened
Virus Vaccines

Most scientists believe that a live virus or weakened virus is not acceptable for use against HIV. Live viruses can replicate, so there is a concern that a live virus vaccine could cause disease. Any virus used must not be capable of causing infection by integrating its genetic material in a host cell. HIV has the ability to change its genetic material. The weakened virus might continue to mutate and reproduce HIV or another virus that is even stronger or more devastating.

Killed (Inactivated)
Virus Vaccines

A whole-killed virus looks just like a live virus, and the immune system recognizes it as such. Early in vaccine research, inactivated whole viruses were thought to be poor candidates for vaccine development. Then, encouraging results with this method in monkeys caused scientists to change their minds. Tests on infected individuals produced no toxic effects. The problem is how to kill the virus and keep its immune-producing properties. Research in this area is still progressing.

Subunit Vaccine

Another strategy for vaccine development is to use non-replicating antigens or antigen fragments of HIV. They will produce an immune response against the target invader. Viral antigens or fragments of HIV can be produced synthetically. These are known as recombinant proteins or synthetic peptides.

Through genetic engineering, scientists have produced recombinant HIV antigens. They can become recombinant vaccines, which are produced by inserting genes of what they want to copy into other viruses, yeasts, or bacteria. The gene products grow and are collected and purified. The result is a laboratory-made protein. This has been done with several HIV proteins: gp160, p24, gp 120, and p55. A great deal of research is being done in this area to produce a synthetic substance that will cause an immune response without causing disease.

HIV proteins are made up of strings of amino acids or peptides. These can be made in a laboratory. Researchers have produced several of these strings of synthetic HIV peptides. In laboratory experiments, they have produced immune responses. Research is continuing on these substances to find a possible safe vaccine against HIV.

Some researchers have found that certain particles resemble viruses in size and shape. They can become a vaccine carrier system. These laboratory-made proteins carry copies of HIV proteins on their surface. These nonreplicating particles are made from a variety of viruses and yeasts.

Idiotype-Based Vaccines

The body will produce an immune response to any foreign substance. These substances can be laboratory made or natural. It's possible to develop a laboratory-made antibody, or idiotype, that will cause the body to produce antibodies against the original invader, such as HIV. The problem is that the immunity is brief. This strategy works only after exposure to HIV, where the time of exposure can be noted. This might be a strategy for use after an occupational exposure, such as a blood spill or needle stick in a hospital emergency room. Continued research is being done on this type of vaccine.

CHAPTER 8

PREVENTION

THE BIGGEST CHALLENGE OF THE HIV EPIDEMIC IS PREVENTION of the spread of infection. HIV infection does not result from an individual's personal traits, such as race, national origin, gender, or sexual orientation. It results from specific behaviors that put one at risk. These behaviors increase the likelihood of exposure to HIV. With HIV, these behaviors are related to sexual activity, drug use, and certain medical procedures. The medical risks can be medical-related, such as blood transfusions or organ transplantations, or they can be cosmetic, as with body piercing and tattooing.

Prevention involves avoiding or modifying behaviors to eliminate or reduce the risk. We are all sexual beings and, therefore, need to learn how to deal with sexual risks. We all need to avoid substance abuse. Having the facts and skills to reduce the risk of HIV is important for everyone, especially teens and young adults.

You can prevent the spread of HIV by

■ Abstaining from or postponing sexual activity.

■ Having sexual relations only within the context of a mutually faithful relationship with an uninfected partner.

■ Using a latex condom or other barrier from beginning to end during all types of sexual intercourse.

■ Not injecting drugs or, if you are using, never sharing needles.

Sexual Abstinence

The most effective way to protect against the spread of HIV is to refrain from any type of oral, vaginal, or anal sexual intercourse with other people. This is sexual abstinence. Practicing abstinence is a 100 percent guaranteed way of preventing sexually transmitted HIV infection.

There are many reasons to abstain from sex. Some choose to abstain because premarital sex goes against their religious or moral beliefs. Others choose to wait because they do not feel they are emotionally prepared or because they feel that their relationship needs time to grow. For some, the reason is fear. They are concerned about pregnancy and may not be ready to handle the decisions and responsibility of adoption, abortion, or parenthood. Besides the fear of HIV, some are concerned about getting other sexually transmitted diseases, such as syphilis, gonorrhea, herpes, genital warts, or *chlamydia*.

Deciding to have sex or to practice abstinence can be a difficult decision. How do you think others feel about premarital sex and abstinence? Consider discussing it with other people. What do your parents think? What do your teachers or guidance counselors think? What does your minister or rabbi think? What do your friends think? What does your boyfriend or girlfriend think? And most important, what do you think? What is important to you? What do you want in a relationship?

For some, sex may be fun and feel good, but even committed relationships have been spoiled by early sex. For many, early sexual experiences are awkward. When you become intimate with another person, regardless of whether it involves heavy petting with one person or sex with many partners, there is increased vulnerability to abuse, assault, or rape. Avoiding these frightening and harmful situations is the best protection. You may try to say no but not be heard. Just remember, if you are raped or abused it is *never* your fault. If this happens to you, get help; get counseling. Go to a trusted adult. It can really make a difference.

If you have had sex and are no longer a virgin, that doesn't mean you can't stop and practice abstinence again. Some have realized they made a mistake. Others try sex and don't like it. They go back to saying no. Some call this "secondary virginity." Whatever you call it, postponing sex altogether reduces the risk of HIV.

Sticking to Your Decision

Discuss your decision with others, especially your boyfriend or girlfriend. Hopefully both of you feel the same way, but it is not always the case. Make it clear how you feel. You may have to say it several times in different ways to get the message across. It is important to help your boyfriend or girlfriend understand that your decision to say no to sex does not mean you don't like them. You can express your love and affection in ways other than sex.

Give thought to what you do, where you go, and whom you are with. If you always do things alone with your boyfriend or girlfriend, saying no is harder. Go out in groups or double date with other couples. Hang out with friends that feel the same way you do. Avoid being alone in a house or apartment when adults will be gone for a long time. Avoid drinking and using drugs because they will cloud your judgment and make you vulnerable to having sex when you don't want to.

Peer pressure is strong. Some friends may think something's wrong with you for not wanting to have sex. They may call you names or tease you for being a virgin. Don't let this get to you. Stick to your ideas, feelings, and values.

Part of the reason that the pressure is so strong is that it seems that everyone is doing it. TV commercials and print ads often use sex to sell their products. Many TV shows include sexual situations or innuendo. It's hard to find a movie that does not have a sex scene in it. Singers sing about sex; artists paint it; photographers photograph it; and comedians tell jokes about it. But everyone is *not* doing it.

It takes time to get to know a person. Before you decide to have sex with someone, talk about their medical, drug using, and sexual history. And remember, people lie, especially about those things. Several studies have shown that people will lie about their background to get someone to say yes to sex. Because of this, going slow is important. Make sure it is right for you. Make sure you get to know and can trust your partner first. Having the information and skills to know and understand when you are ready will help insure that you have a healthy and responsible sexual relationship.

Don't let your boyfriend or girlfriend pressure you. Pressure to have sex comes from girls *and* boys. Pressure from boys is usually strong and straightforward. "If you don't have sex, I'll leave you." (What they may be thinking instead is "hurt you" or "rape you.") This might be a good time to say good-bye. Girls use more subtle pressure. "You know how much I love you." Your response can be, "Yes, and I love you just as much." Don't fall for lines or feel that love is something you must prove.

One of the best ways of being ready to say no is to practice. Be forceful and assertive when you say no. Say no as soon as possible. Be direct. Be firm. Be calm. Be honest. Be brief. Don't apologize. Look the person in the eye. Look as if you mean it. Use a clear, firm voice. Don't make up excuses. How would you respond to the pressure from others?

Good refusal skills are techniques you can use to reinforce your decision to say no. Some hints include the following:

- As you speak, look directly into the other person's eyes.

- Provide alternatives.

- Show you care about the other person and about yourself.

- Take definite action.

- Speak in a forceful but calm manner.

Choosing to Be Sexually Active

Most people, at some time, choose to be sexually active. If you do so, limit the number of partners you have. The more partners you have, the greater the risk of HIV infection. Get to know the person. Choose your partners carefully because one infected person is all it takes. Unfortunately, there are *monogamous* individuals who were infected by their partners. If you or your partner has been sexually active or has used drugs, maybe both of you should get HIV tested before having sex.

If you do choose to be sexually active, there are three types of decisions you can make about your sexual behav-

Responses To Common Lines

IF HE/SHE SAYS	YOU CAN SAY
Lots of kids in school are doing it!	Then you should have an easy time finding a partner!
Don't you want me?	I want what is right for both of us.
You can prove you love me by having sex with me.	You can prove you love me by not pressuring me to do something I don't want to do.
Why do you keep saying no?	Because that is how I feel. What part of the word NO don't you understand?
It is not such a big deal.	Then I want to wait until it is a big deal for me.
I know plenty of people that would love to get to bed with me.	Then maybe you are going out with the wrong person.
I have to have sex to release the pressure inside.	Go into the bathroom and use your hand. You don't need me for that.
Everyone is doing it.	That's not true. I'm not!
It's fun.	No! It's not fun to do the wrong thing.
You said yes once before.	It's my right to say NO anytime I want to, even if I said yes before!
It makes you more mature.	No! Mature means making good decisions, not doing things with serious consequences.

ior. You can practice *safe sex*. You can practice *safer sex*. Or you can practice *unsafe sex*.

Safe Sex

Intimacy and closeness between lovers is important. Even though you have decided not to have sexual intercourse, it doesn't mean you can't have fun. It doesn't mean you cannot express love and affection. Safe sex is any nonpenetrative sexual behavior that does not expose a person to another individual's blood, semen, *vaginal secretions* or breast milk on or near the anus, vagina, mouth, urethra or into an opening in the skin. Some people call safe sex "*outercourse*."

Deciding how far to go is not easy. Talk to your friends, boyfriends, girlfriends, parents or other trusted adults. All of the following activities are safe and won't spread HIV: hugging, kissing, massage, petting, body-to-body rubbing, manual stimulation, partner masturbation. There are many ways to be loving without having sex. Look at the list on page 99. Can you think of others?

Safer Sex

Sex with a condom or other latex barrier, such as a *dental dam*, is safer sex. It is called safer sex because it is safer than intercourse without a condom. It does *not* provide 100 percent protection from HIV, other sexually transmitted diseases or pregnancy, but it is safer. In fact, when condoms are used correctly and consistently, people are protected close to 98 percent of the time.[1] But they need to be used correctly all the time to get this protection.

Deciding to be sexually active is not easy. Unlike on TV or in the movies, most people do not just jump into bed. For a sexual experience to be rewarding, it takes planning and thought. Talk to your partner. What is their risk of HIV? What is their medical history? Have they had other partners? How many? All this may sound embarrassing and hard to

99 Ways to Make Love Without Having Sex!

1. Say I love you
2. Hug
3. Kiss
4. Send flowers
5. Hold hands
6. Have deep, meaningful conversations
7. Treat each other nice
8. Smile at each other
9. Write a poem
10. Dance together
11. Talk about feelings
12. Discuss problems
13. Be together
14. Go out
15. Say, "I don't want to be with anyone else"
16. Go to a drive-in
17. Ask, "How are you feeling"
18. Sort out disagreements
19. Give a back rub
20. Let him do your hair

21. Put up with their friends
22. Go to a concert together
23. Give gifts
24. Play pool
25. Observe the stars together
26. Share same hobbies
27. Give a kiss on the ear
28. Whisper, "I love you"
29. Be nice to each other
30. Give a token from the heart
31. Visit the other person's parents
32. Write love letters
33. Call to say hello or good night
34. Blow kisses
35. Give a ring or other jewelry
36. Go to someplace meaningful or special
37. Have a romantic picnic in the park
38. Show affection

39. Talk about the reasons for the decision to wait to have sex

40. Buy something nice for the other person

41. Go swimming together

42. Go hiking together

43. Be their best friend

44. Sit and talk a long time

45. Share thoughts

46. Go skating

47. Sing a song

48. Do things you two used to do when you first met

49. Ask to be with each other more

50. Build a strong relationship

51. Do housework and chores together

52. Communicate

53. Say, "I care"

54. Caress each other

55. Stick up for each other when in trouble

56. Say, "I'll always be there for you"

57. Be sensitive

58. Listen

59. Go out of the way for each other

60. Go camping

61. Say, "I appreciate how you treat me"

62. Respect each other

63. Buy something special or sentimental

64. Help by carrying things

65. Play miniature golf

66. Take a walk together

67. Go to a party

68. Cook for each other

69. Just touch each other

70. Leave a love note

71. Dedicate a favorite song on the radio

72. Say, "I love you" in another language

73. Say that good things are worth waiting for

74. Go back to the place you first met

75. Watch each other play sports

76. Spend a day at a carnival or fair
77. Eat at a romantic restaurant with elegant music and a dance floor
78. Do homework together
79. Pay attention to the other's likes and dislikes
80. Make the other person comfortable
81. Draw a heart with both names in it
82. Treat the other person like royalty
83. Send a card
84. Talk on the phone
85. Hold each other close
86. Trust each other
87. Support each other
88. Go for a drive
89. Go skiing
90. Sit real close while watching a movie
91. Take care of each other when sick
92. Make a present
93. Go to a sporting event
94. Carry the other's picture
96. Cuddle
97. Watch a sunset or sunrise together
98. Be faithful
99. Share secrets

do, but it's not as hard as living with AIDS. A sincere partner will appreciate your honesty and finding out about you. Make sure you're comfortable with their answers. Remember, people do lie, especially about sex and drugs.

Tell your partner that you want and plan to use condoms or dental dams. Decide who is going to get them. What kind will you use? Do you or your partner know how to use them properly, or is it the first time for one or both of you? If it is, where can you go for help? What will you do if the condom breaks? What if she gets pregnant?

Condoms

A condom is a sheath that covers the penis. It protects against many sexually transmitted diseases, including HIV infection. It works by acting as a barrier to keep semen, vaginal fluid, and blood from passing from one person to another.

Condoms are available in supermarkets, pharmacies, and other stores. Many community agencies and health centers distribute free condoms. They are also available from vending machines, but vending machine condoms are often the least reliable and should be purchased with caution. Machines can be subject to extreme heat and cold, and the condoms may have been in the machine for a long time.

Although most condoms look alike, there are differences. The first step in choosing a condom is to read the label. Look for the following:

■   Condoms should be made of latex (rubber). Some condoms are made of natural membrane, such as lambskin, but these natural condoms have small microscopic holes, like pores in your skin. The holes are small enough to keep sperm in and prevent pregnancy, but they let HIV and other sexually transmitted diseases through.

■   The package should say that the condoms are for disease prevention. Novelty condoms, like ones that glow in the dark, should not be used. If they are used, they should be used on top of a latex condom that provides disease prevention protection.

■   The package should have a manufacture date. Those with *spermicide* should have an expiration date. The condom should not be purchased or used after the expiration date, and don't buy a condom more than two years after the manufacture date.

Condoms help protect you against many sexually transmitted diseases, including HIV infection.

■ Some condoms come in different colors. The color of a condom doesn't matter, but using different colors can add to the fun. If the colored condoms come in foil packages, you may be surprised with the color you get.

■ Spermicides kill sperm cells and many sexually transmitted diseases. *Nonoxynol-9* is the most common spermicide on condoms. In laboratory tests, it has been shown to kill HIV. Nonoxynol-9 has a bitter taste. So if the condom is going to be used for oral sex, getting a condom without a spermicide may be best. Some people are allergic to nonoxynol-9. If you or your partner is allergic, pick a different condom.

■ Some condoms are lubricated and some are dry. Lubrication helps keep condoms from breaking. If you buy a nonlubricated condom and need to add lubrication, make sure it is water based (like K-Y Jelly®) and not oil based. Oil-based lubricants—such as petroleum jelly, baby oil or lotion, hand cream, cooking oil, or oily cosmetics—will cause latex to tear easily.

■ Condoms come in different shapes. Some have a tip or reservoir. This is the best choice. The tip forms a place for the semen to go after the man ejaculates. It prevents the fluid from blowing up the condom and causing breakage. Some condoms also have ridges that add stimulation for the woman during intercourse.

Condoms should be stored in a cool dry place. Do not leave them in your car where the temperature can reach more than 100°F (38°C) in the sun or drop below freezing in the winter. These extreme temperatures destroy the condom. Never keep condoms in your wallet or back pocket. Squashing and sitting on them will break the condoms.

Handle the package gently. Don't use teeth, sharp fingernails, scissors, or other sharp objects. They may damage the condom. Make sure you can see what you are doing. Don't open condoms in the dark. Inspect the condom after opening. If it sticks to itself or is brittle, it is not good. Don't use it.

The following guidelines are suggested to ensure that the condom is used properly for disease prevention. Remember: No condom is 100 percent effective. Following these guidelines will increase the chances of its success. Most condom

Condom Shopping Guide

Use this handy shopping guide as a reminder of what to look for when buying condoms, lubricants and spermicide.

Be sure to check for:

✔ Latex

✔ Disease prevention claim on package label

✔ Expiration date: do not use expired condoms

Also consider:

✔ Reservoir tip

✔ With spermicide (Nonoxynol-9)

✔ Separate spermicide

   – Gel

   – Cream

   – Foam

✔ With lubricant

✔ Separate lubricant

✔ Stored in cool dry place

failure comes from not using it properly, not manufacturer defect. If you are under the influence of drugs or alcohol, it will interfere with your ability to function properly.

1. Use a new condom every time you have intercourse. Never reuse a condom.

2. Be careful of sharp objects, such as fingernails, rings, other jewelry, or braces on your teeth. They can tear the condom.

3. If the penis is not circumcised, pull the foreskin back before putting on the condom.

4. Put the condom on after the penis is erect and before any contact is made between the penis and any part of the partner's body.

5. If using extra spermicide, put some inside the condom tip and on the outside of the condom.

6. While pinching the tip, place the condom on the tip of the penis and unroll it all the way to the base of the penis.

7. If the condom does not have a reservoir tip, pinch the tip enough to leave a half-inch space for semen to collect.

8. If you feel the condom break during intercourse, stop immediately and withdraw. Do not continue until you put on a new condom and use spermicide.

9. After ejaculation and before the penis becomes limp, grip the base of the condom and withdraw carefully while you hold onto the condom.

10. To remove the condom, gently pull it off the penis, being careful that semen does not spill out.

11. Wrap the used condom in a tissue and throw it in the trash. Do not flush it down the toilet, as it may clog the plumbing.

Condoms only work when you use them. People often come up with all kinds of objections and reasons not to use a condom. How would you respond if you heard some of these common objections?

How to Put on a Condom

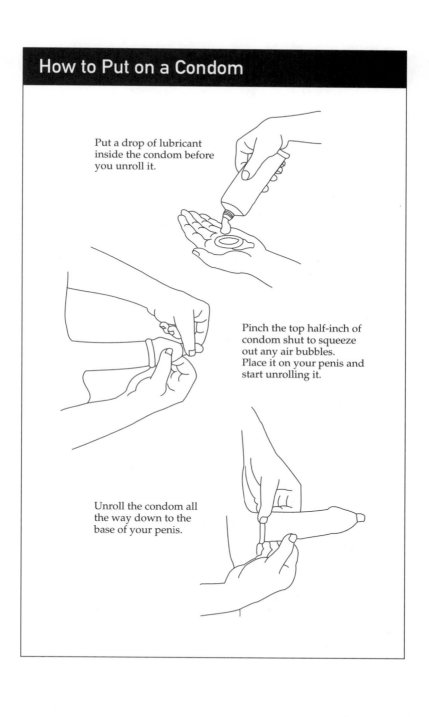

Put a drop of lubricant inside the condom before you unroll it.

Pinch the top half-inch of condom shut to squeeze out any air bubbles. Place it on your penis and start unrolling it.

Unroll the condom all the way down to the base of your penis.

- You can't feel anything; they take away sensitivity.
- Men lose their erections while putting them on.
- They take away from the spontaneity of sex.
- They're too tight; I'm too big.
- They interrupt the rhythm of lovemaking.
- They're awkward.
- They're messy.
- They're expensive; I can't afford them.
- My partner refuses to use them.
- My partner is clean.
- My partner would be suspicious or accuse me of cheating.
- My partner would leave me.
- My partner would be abusive.
- Sex is the one thing I can control; using condoms takes away that control.
- Condoms are for avoiding pregnancy, and I want to have children.
- Using condoms is against my religion.
- Ejaculating inside a woman is the only real way to have sex. I don't want a woman who won't take my semen.
- Sex is not enjoyable with a condom.
- They're not 100 percent effective, why should I use them?

Here are some sample responses to some of these objections. See how many responses you can come up with. The more you practice and think about how you would respond, the easier it will be for you to be assertive and stay in control.

Responses to Partners Not Wanting to Use Condoms

IF PARTNER SAYS	YOU CAN SAY
I don't have a condom with me.	The supermarket is open all night. Let's go and get some. OR Let's wait until we have one.
Putting on a condom breaks the mood. It's not romantic.	I think it can be very romantic. Let me show you…I'll put it on you.
Condoms taste terrible.	Lets try some of the new flavored condoms.
But you said you loved me!	I do love you. That's why I want to protect us.
I never use condoms!	I never have sex without them. I guess you will have to be with someone else.
They are too dry and make sex uncomfortable.	Lets use lubricanted condoms, and we can add extra K-Y Jelly. I am sure that will feel better.

The Female Condom

In the past, condoms were only worn by men. Now there is another alternative. There is a female condom that can be worn inside the vagina and conforms to the shape of the body. It can be inserted up to eight hours before intercourse, but most women who use it will insert it a few minutes before sex. It has been designed to help prevent pregnancy and prevent sexually transmitted diseases including HIV infection. It serves as a barrier to block the passage of semen into the vagina.

Female condoms are made of thin plastic and have two rings. One ring is at the bottom, and the other is at the top. The bottom ring is inserted into the vagina like a diaphragm. The top ring remains outside the body for easy removal.

If a woman is using a female condom, her male partner should *not* use a latex condom. This could prevent both products from staying in place.

A female condom helps prevent pregnancy and many sexually transmitted diseases.

Use more lubricant if needed. The lubricant can be placed on the outside of the condom before insertion, on the inside of the condom, or directly on the man's penis. Added lubrication may make use more comfortable and may allow the penis to move more easily in and out of the vagina.

To insert a female condom, find a comfortable position. Stand with one foot on a chair or the toilet, or sit with knees apart, or squat down. Make sure the inner ring is at the bottom of the condom. Hold the condom with the open end hanging down. Squeeze the inner ring and insert it into the vagina. Add an extra amount of lubricant to make it easier. Push the condom all the way up into the vagina so the inner ring is past the pubic bone and up against the cervix. Make sure the condom is inserted straight and not twisted. The outer ring should lie on the outer labia of the vagina. About one inch of the condom will be sticking out of the vagina. After intercourse, twist and squeeze the outer ring to keep semen inside. Pull it out gently and throw it in the trash. *Do not reuse and do not flush it down the toilet.*

Dental Dams

Oral sex can spread HIV. A dental dam is a flat sheet of latex used by a dentist when operating on a tooth. It can be used during oral sex as a barrier. The dental dam is placed over the vaginal canal and prevents vaginal fluid from getting into the partner's mouth. Dental dams can be purchased in many drugstores. If a dental dam is not available, one can be made by cutting a latex condom into a flat sheet.

Unsafe Sex

The riskiest sexual behavior is unsafe sex. This is oral, anal, or vaginal sexual intercourse without the use of a condom or other latex barrier. Intercourse without the use of a condom puts one at risk of HIV infection.

Putting on a Female Condom

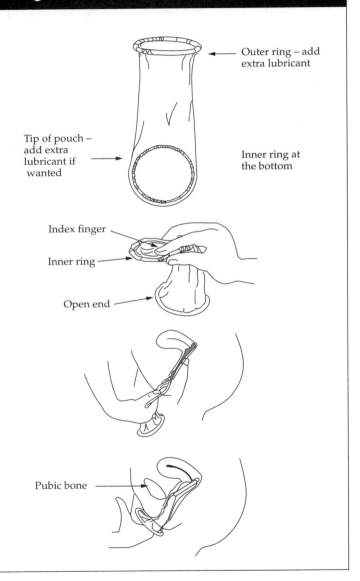

Outer ring – add
extra lubricant

Tip of pouch –
add extra
lubricant if
wanted

Inner ring at
the bottom

Index finger

Inner ring

Open end

Pubic bone

Drugs and Needles

Using drugs or alcohol clouds your thinking. People under the influence don't make good decisions. The best way to prevent a problem is by staying in control. Say no to drugs and alcohol. This is often not an easy decision, because so many parties and places serve alcohol. Are the parties in your community like that? What could you do to change things, so parties are safe but still fun?

Get Help

If you are already using drugs or alcohol and cannot stop by yourself, get help. You don't have to go through it alone. Your parents, guidance counselors, family doctor, clergy, or other adult can help. There are clinics that will help you. Thousands of other people like yourself have been helped to stop.

Don't Use Needles

If you cannot stop, do not use needles. Besides HIV, needle use puts you at risk for hepatitis B and the risk of overdosing on the drug. Drug habits are expensive, especially when using the quantity required by a needle-using addict. Using needles puts you at risk of stealing or having sex to pay for your habit. All these are good reasons not to use needles. Can you think of others?

Clean Needles

HIV infection can be transmitted by sharing needles used to inject drugs. If you must use needles because you are addicted and cannot stop, *do not share a needle or works with anyone.* Some clinics and agencies give away needles to addicts so addicts won't be forced to share them with others to get the drugs they need. Others have needle-exchange programs. At these programs, addicts bring in their dirty needle and will get a clean one in exchange. Research shows that

How to Clean Needles to Help Prevent the Spread of HIV

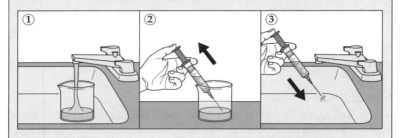

A. First wash out needle with clean water
  - Repeat steps 2 and 3 three times
  - Shake and tap syringe before emptying

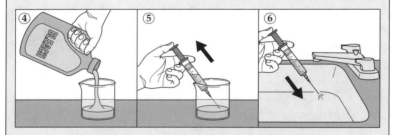

B. Then disinfect with bleach
  - Repeat steps 5 and 6 three times
  - Shake and tap syringe before emptying

C. Repeat water washing steps to clean out bleach

needle-exchange programs help reduce HIV infection, and they do not cause a rise in drug use as some people feared.

If you must share needles, clean them first. Assume that anyone who shoots drugs may be HIV infected. Protect yourself by cleaning the needles and works before you use them. In an informal poll done with hundreds of high school students, finding a class without a student who didn't know a friend or family member who used needles was hard. Even if these students were not using needles themselves, they needed to know how to clean needles to help their friends. If your friend or family member was using needles, could you show them how to clean a needle to stay HIV safe while they were trying to stop?

Cleaning needles and works with full-strength bleach is important. It reduces the risk of HIV transmission. Before using bleach, wash out the needle and syringe by filling it with water several times. This reduces the amount of blood left in the syringe. Shaking and tapping the syringe is recommended when it is filled with wash water, with bleach, and with rinse water. Shaking improves the effectiveness of each step.

CHAPTER 9

YVETTE'S STORY

[Note to the reader: Yvette's story is a true story about her life. It is told in her own words. It reflects her experiences and feelings about living with HIV and the events that led up to being infected.]

My name is Yvette. I am 26, and I am HIV infected.

I grew up around the Woodstock, New York, area. I spent a lot of time in the mountains and with nature. It was a beautiful place to grow up. When I think about my childhood, I now realize the powerful emotional impact it had on my life. There were happy things about my childhood, but there were also very scary things.

My parents lived a 1970s hippie lifestyle. We lived with a lot of people. No one really had a steady job in those days. When I was two, my parents were divorced. So, for a long time, it was just my mother, my brother, and me. My mom was a poet. She read poetry in local coffeehouses and worked for an antiques dealer.

I was a very shy, withdrawn kid. There was a lot of drug use in my family. Sometimes I felt I wasn't part of society. I knew I couldn't talk with other kids at school or with any adult about what was going on in my house. I was always afraid that my parents were going to be arrested and taken away. There wouldn't be anyone to take care of me.

In those days there were many people around us living that lifestyle. So, on the one hand it seemed normal. On the other hand, I knew there was something strange and different about it.

I was sexually abused by my mother's father until I was a teenager. So I felt very alienated from other kids at school and had a hard time making friends. I didn't really understand what was going on. It was all very confusing.

Everyone has good and bad qualities. Some of the things I really loved about my mother were that she was well educated and creative. She passed that on to us. She read to us every night. She would take us to the ballet in New York City.

I learned to read when I was very young, and I love to read. I spent many hours of my free time reading. I loved learning about other cultures and music and mythology.

I loved the rural environment. I loved the fall and the changing colors. I loved to go hiking and being able to go swimming in the lake. There were a lot fewer people there then. I am grateful for having lived in that quiet environment, something I realize now after having lived in several cities.

After high school, I studied filmmaking in California. Then I moved to Dallas for a year, where I worked in a law office. Following that, I lived and went to college in New Orleans. I loved it there, even though it was a violent city. I also lived in Manhattan for a short time. It was very stressful for me there. I go on sensory overload whenever I go back there.

I like where I live now. It's a small suburban-type city. I have access to many things. I am trying to keep my life as simple as possible. My apartment is close to the store and the post office. It's a city, but I can see the trees from my window. The support groups I go to are not too far away.

For the most part, people around here have been very supportive. I was surprised how much support I have gotten. My family has been supportive. Most of my acquaintances are part of one *twelve-step program* or another, so they tend to be open-minded.

When I first moved here, I didn't know anyone and was afraid to talk about my HIV status. Then I heard one person talk about it, and I decided to see how it would go. It really felt hard to hold everything in. Many emotions go along with what happened to me. Not to talk about it gets overwhelming. When I started talking about it, around six months ago, people thought I was very brave. I have talked to student peer leaders and to troubled youth in a halfway house.

Yet, I can't tell everyone. My boyfriend's mother has been most difficult. She is concerned in general for her son. It is not personal against me. It is understandable but very painful. We have been going out for a little over a year. Actually she doesn't know my HIV status. We decided not to tell her. There were times when I was sick and reacting badly to new medications. She was very protective of her son. I guess sometimes it is better not tell someone, if you know they can't handle it. It is uncomfortable, because I love him very much, and it hurts to know we're keeping a secret.

Telling my father was very hard. We have continued a relationship. He lives in Florida now and teaches English to gifted high school students. He has remarried. We haven't been real close over the years. But we maintained brief contact through letters. When I went into recovery two years ago, I told him I had a problem with drugs and alcohol.

Our relationship started to get better. I knew I was HIV positive, but I didn't know how to tell him. Getting to know someone you didn't know for a long time was strange. It was really scary to have to tell him. So I waited about four months. Then I wrote him a letter and told him what happened. He called the day he got the letter and said he would be up to see me in three days. He drove here from Florida and spent a week. It was really an incredible experience. He was sad but very supportive. I think he was in shock at first. Then, as time went on, he started to ask me medical things. Now, he keeps track of medical treatments and always calls me.

Telling my older brother was also hard. He is in college now. My little brother and sister still don't know. I just don't know how to tell them. They knew some people who died of AIDS, and I think they would be too scared if they found out now.

When I speak to groups, I don't always tell about being abused. I usually say I came from a very dysfunctional household. When I went to high school, I was very rebellious. I felt I wasn't getting love and support from my family. The structure just wasn't there. I didn't have any discipline. I was allowed to do whatever I wanted. So I was very wild. I did a lot of very risky behaviors. I can't say that it was all because of being abused. But it was surely a part of it.

When my parents got divorced, we lived with my grandparents. So from age two to five we lived with them. When we moved out of their place, we would still go back and visit on weekends and holidays. So then it was happening on weekends and holidays.

My abuse was a major contributor to my addiction. I started using when I was five years old. I had nightmares. I couldn't sleep. So my mother started giving me Valium®. By the time I was eight or nine, I was completely dependent upon sleeping pills. Without them, I couldn't sleep at night because I was so terrified. It was a way to keep my memories back and my anger under control. I sedated my anger.

All this has come out over the years. At age 12, I started talking about what happened. I was very vocal about it. I have a little sister who is now seven. When she was born, I became very adamant with my mother about what happened to me. I didn't want it to happen to her. I said I didn't ever want her left alone with him, or I would get her taken away. That was my way of dealing with what happened to me. I was really afraid it would happen to her too.

At least now I have grown and know what was going on. When I was young, I didn't understand. It all stopped though when I was 12 and got my period. He was probably afraid to get me pregnant. Maybe I was too old for him. He may have been afraid of a girl who was beginning to mature.

At age 12, I started drinking. This was along with the pill habit I had. I became very wild. For a long time I was in denial about my drug problem. I saw many people use every day and still have a job and go to school. I didn't think I was a nonfunctional addict. I worked. I went to school. I got straight A's. I did very well, and all this time I was using drugs and drinking. This was especially true at Loyola College, where I was a women's studies major.

When I first moved to New Orleans, I used very little. I occasionally smoked pot and later started drinking. At first, I was in a relationship. I was going to school full time and working full time. I kept my life very full. My feelings about the past, however, started coming out. In my relationship, I obviously had a sexual dysfunction. I was frigid. So I went to therapy for about six months for the incest. After the six months, it got so frightening to me. My post-traumatic stress symptoms started to happen. I thought I was going crazy. I started having panic attacks and blackouts. I guess I wasn't ready to deal with going to therapy, so I stopped.

I might have actually been HIV infected when I was in New Orleans. As part of that monogamous relationship I did get tested. It was negative. That wasn't the first time I was tested. I had lived in the same house with my mother's friends who had AIDS. There was no chance of getting infected then. But I got tested anyway. It was early in the epidemic, and I was worried about getting it casually. Now I know that was stupid thinking.

Anyway, when I left that relationship in New Orleans, I started drinking again. I then had an affair with this guy who was a crack addict from a really bad neighborhood in New Orleans. I wasn't using with him, but I slept with him. Sometimes we used a condom, and sometimes we didn't. I didn't get tested while with him. I guess I was afraid that I had been infected from him. I knew he had many sexual partners, and they were mostly addicts who also had many sexual partners.

When I got back from New Orleans about four years ago, I had a miscarriage and went back into therapy. All that stuff was still there in my head. Plus, I was seeing my family, because they still lived in New York. They hadn't moved to Florida yet. Seeing my sister brought up a lot of stuff. She was the same age as I was when I was abused. She even looked like me. I wasn't using at that point, but my psychiatrist prescribed medication. I was now taking Prozac®.

My mother was very much in denial about what happened. When she started going to therapy, she had a nervous breakdown. She has a lot of very self-destructive behavior also. Seeing that was very painful for me. I was getting better, and I was looking at her. It was hard for me. All that stuff was coming up, and I became enraged.

It was the first time in my life that I started to feel this incredible rage for what had happened to me and because my family had not protected me. I was angry at my mother and stepfather for having my brother and sister in what I considered an unsafe situation. I was just furious. They say that men and women deal with abuse differently. Men usually end up being external, and they become abusers. And women take it out on themselves. I did that. I started breaking things in my apartment. I felt very uncomfortable having that kind of violent behavior. I started to cut myself. Then, I stopped taking the Prozac and eventually started taking other drugs again.

My therapist noticed that I was coming to sessions high. She would say, "You should go to AA." I would say, "No, that's not my problem. My problem is my family and what happened to me. I am OK." I was back in denial! But at that point, I was so aware of my feelings and nothing was working. I was smoking pot, having nightmares again, and having flashbacks of the abuse.

By this time I was 24. I moved to New York City. Amazingly, I still hadn't ever used needles. I was working with this guy who was a heroin addict. I guess for a long time I had a fear of needles. But the other drugs I was doing were not strong enough. They were not erasing my feelings. I was still remembering, still having the flashbacks. I needed something stronger. So that was when I thought about it. I thought about it for a long time. And finally I asked my friend to give me some. Up to that time I was afraid to use a needle because I was aware of the risks. My mother had many very close friends who had contracted AIDS. One of them was my godfather. He had already died. Another was a woman who was like my surrogate mother. I had stayed with her whenever I had nowhere else to stay. I had known her since I was 9 or 10 years old, and now she was dying. Her husband had already died of AIDS. All these people were very close to me, so I was afraid of using a needle because I knew it would increase the risk.

But when it got to that point, I didn't care anymore. It was like getting addicted wasn't going to happen to me. I was only going to do it this once. I wanted just to see what it was like. It was twisted thinking.

I think at that point I was so angry and so depressed, I wasn't thinking rationally at all about my safety. I really didn't care about myself anymore. So I used a needle for three months.

Being aware that this can happen to anyone is really important. I am sure that most kids have some type of unsafe behavior. Before I used a needle, I had a lot of unsafe sex. I can't be 100 percent sure how I got HIV. I could have gotten it from sex without using a condom.

I would say be aware, be tested regularly. It is no joke. We live in a different time now than our parents. That was then, and this is now. This is a very real thing.

You don't have to wait until things get overwhelming. You can ask for help about what is going on in your family. You don't have to escape to the streets. There is help available. There is a lot of support. I didn't want to ask for help, because I didn't believe that anybody really cared for me. I found this to be far from the truth. There is so much help and so much support.

Much of the behavior that causes HIV infection is related to drinking and drugs. If you are at a party and you had too much to drink and a girl asks you to use a condom, you might not use it. But, if you were sober, you might think about it.

I know from experience that when you are in that lifestyle, you are not thinking. What I really want to say is that most kids are going to have experiences in life using substances. Some will not touch it, but a lot will. You just can't predict what your behavior is going to be like when you are under the influence of a substance. I would stress that if you know you are going to be at a party or going somewhere where you are likely to be in an altered state, always have condoms with you and always use them.

If a guy wants to sleep with you and won't use a condom, that means he doesn't respect you. It means he doesn't care about you or about himself. If you think about that, it may make it easier to say no.

I don't know how many teens are going to end up using a needle. There are needle-exchange programs. If you are going to share a needle, you can get a new one instead. Or you can sterilize it with bleach and water. It only takes a few minutes, and the virus will die. If you are going to use needles, there are ways to protect yourself from HIV. My problem was that I wasn't aware of them. When I started to use, I didn't know about needle-exchange programs. If I had, I would have taken advantage of them.

Needles are sold on the street. They come in a plastic package. They are usually sold right near where you get drugs. Many people buy them for three dollars. You are told they are new, but they are really used. Addicts will package them as new needles. It is especially dangerous for new users. They don't know where to go for needles. The people who are selling them are trying to raise money for their own habit. This is a common practice. I would never trust a needle bought on the street to be a clean needle.

I think many users are really afraid. Most users will clean their needles when they have the stuff and are taught how. IV drug users are at the highest risk of HIV infection. With needle use, you are definitely getting someone else's blood injected into your veins. It is a sure way to get HIV.

I know people in recovery. When they talk about their using days, they did clean needles, but not always. I remember once when I was in the city for almost three months, the health department set up a booth where they were giving out bleach kits. When I got it, I started to clean the needle.

At that point, though, I guess I was already infected. I didn't know for sure, but I suspected it. I wasn't too conscious of what I was doing. I had been using needles then for about two months. Probably, if I was tested at that point, I wouldn't have tested positive yet. It was very early in my infection.

About a month later, I did go through the acute stage of the virus. I had the flulike symptoms, and I got boils on my face that looked like chicken pox. So I went through that first stage of the illness about three months after I started using needles.

I didn't have enough money to get drugs, but I didn't really have a very big habit. I took some of what my partner was using. I do not think I ever did a whole bag of heroin. Most people will do three bags at a time if they have a heavy habit. I never did a whole bag. I was very sensitive to it. It was not something I could have sustained for very long. I did not take to it very well. In fact, I was really miserable when I was using. Toward the end, when I was starting to get cravings, I would go out and steal.

I would steal books and sell them to people on the street who have booths that sell books and perfume and stuff. I would usually get enough for one bag. But I was constantly having to do that. The high didn't last very long. I would go out and steal every day for about two months. I also worked. I had a full-time job in which I managed to do quite well. Surprisingly, they didn't suspect what was going on with my habit. So I had my paycheck also.

I am not really sure that I got HIV from the needles. There were those guys in New Orleans. I was also having unprotected sex with my partner, the person I was sharing needles with. We lived together for about six months. At that point, I thought of him as my boyfriend, but I am not sure how much of an intimate relationship it really was.

He is positive now but didn't get tested until I called him and told him I was positive. I can speculate that he knew, but I don't know for sure. I don't know how he is now. He was sicker than I am and was still using after I stopped. I stopped when I found out. That's why I stopped. I pray that he is doing well.

This last test was really scary because I think I knew I was positive. The others were slightly scary, but before, I didn't think I was positive. At least it wasn't scary until the day I was supposed to get the results. Then, as I was sitting in the chair, it was very suspenseful. When they finally said, "negative," I would give a sigh of relief and say, "I knew it was going to be negative!" It was really scary in those few moments because they have to take you into the room and tell you confidentially. If they would just call you up and say it was negative and you didn't have to come in, it would feel better. I guess just having to go through the whole process was scarier than I want to admit.

The last time was scary, but it wasn't because I really knew. I had psyched myself up for it already. Though it is scary, getting tested is very important.

All this happened when I was 24. Now I am 26. It was quite an amazing two years. It has been the most wonderful two years of my life. Because, when I found out that I was HIV positive, I completely changed my life.

Life was meaningless to me before that. I was . . . I didn't care! I didn't see life as a gift. When I got my diagnosis, suddenly I started to realize how serious it was. I wanted to live. I started to change my life. The first thing I did was stop using drugs by going to a twelve-step program. I started to look for a better way. I tried to let go of my anger towards my family and society. It has been a really beautiful journey to open up to a positive way of life. I guess it is ironic that HIV is what it took. But if that is what it took, that's OK!

My new boyfriend lives down the street. We lived together for about two months. Both of us are early in recovery. It is a process. In the first few years of recovery you really get to know yourself. You can get distracted in relationships. So we decided to live apart for a while. But I think that's good. He works hard and has a busy schedule.

My boyfriend is a really good person. He is warm and gentle. For me, it is wonderful to know that I don't have to settle for someone just because I have HIV infection. He plays the piano. He is the kind of person you deserve. I met him in recovery. He was my dream guy. It is incredible. I used to go back a lot and say, "Well, if I had just come to recovery three months earlier and met him earlier, I wouldn't have been HIV positive." But I don't do that anymore. I just try to stay in the moment of what I have now. I don't look back. I am very grateful.

Yet the truth is that our relationship is painful sometimes because of the HIV. Sometimes he is in a little bit of denial about it. He used to go to a support group for partners with HIV, but he has stopped going. He feels that I am not sick because I am taking protease inhibitors and feeling good. He thinks he doesn't need to go. I don't know whether that is true or whether dealing with it all the time is just painful. It is easy for both of us, now that I am feeling healthy, to sort of push it away. But I think that attending a support group is very important.

Still, we always have safer sex, so it never really goes away. There were two times since we have been together that the condom broke. It was horrifying. You're suddenly hit with the fact that it isn't 100 percent effective.

I am always taking my medication. I have to take it every eight hours and other stuff in between. I have to eat a certain way. We can never ignore it. With the protease inhibitor, you have to take it on an empty stomach, and you have to take it three times a day at the exact time. So there is a three-hour period in each part of the day when you can't eat.

I have found that to keep my immune system healthy, I have to eat really healthy. What I take into my body really affects me. I can feel the difference. I try not to eat too much sugar and caffeine, because that depletes the immune system. I try to eat many vegetables and grains. I haven't eaten meat most of my life. I do a lot of juicing—beet juice and carrot juice are great for the immune system.

I feel a total difference in the way I function when I eat sugar and carbohydrates and caffeine compared with drinking juices and eating a healthy meal. With healthy food, I feel great. I get plenty of energy. I will be in a good mood and can go on with my daily life. If I have a donut for breakfast or have candy at break time or eat fatty foods for lunch, I cannot function. I am extremely tired, cranky, and feel blah. I have to come home and take a nap.

Now I take AZT, 3TC, and the protease inhibitor Crixivan®. Luckily I haven't had any opportunistic infections yet. It got to the point last winter, when I was very sick. My T cells were dropping. They were down to 270. I lost a lot of weight and was not able to gain it back.

I started to have thrush and night sweats. That's when I first started taking medication. At first I was very resistant to taking medication. But after two weeks of having thrush and night sweats, I said, "Give me something!" I was really scared. To see my T cells getting down to the 200 mark was scary. They just kept dropping.

When I was first positive, they were at 570. They were steadily dropping. I was trying to take the best care of myself that I could, but it wasn't doing anything. So I started taking medication. The AZT and 3TC helped a little, but the protease inhibitor is the real miracle drug. Now my T cells are at 400 and my blood viral load is undetectable.

Now that I am feeling better, I really want to study HIV law and help people with their legal issues. My next step is to get a paralegal certificate. Maybe I will go on from there. I have thought about doing HIV counseling. I think I might be more helpful with law than with counseling. I can get too emotionally involved with people. I am kind of co-dependent. With legal aspects, I can stay a little bit removed. It is more intellectual, and I am very good at that kind of thing. I am very organized.

I keep thinking how different my life is now. It is just amazing! After my diagnosis, I wrote a series of poems about Persephone. In Greek mythology, she was abducted by Pluto, god of the underworld. I felt like that was a way of living with the idea of my mortality.

I have even thought about having a baby. My boyfriend has talked about having children someday. I would want to have the sperm injected in me, so we won't have to have unsafe sex. With my low viral load and with AZT, there is only a very small chance of transmission. But do I even want to take that small chance? It is a hard decision. I have also thought about nursing. I think it is more healthy for the baby, but it probably won't be safe. I want my baby to live a long healthy life.

Many people around me have died of AIDS. Someday I would like to make a quilt for one of them, an old friend of my mom. When I came back from New York City and went into recovery, I didn't have anywhere safe to stay. Everyone I knew was an active addict. My mom's friend opened his home to me. He had AIDS. He was in his last stage. I stayed with him for about four months. He died about a year ago. Every time I think of it, I get overwhelmed.

I guess someday, I would like a quilt made for me. I would want my brother and sister to write about me or put something on it. It is hard to know how they would feel. They are very artistic and would make a beautiful quilt. I think I would want a picture of a cat on the quilt. I love cats. My boyfriend has a cat. We share it. I love that cat. I would want lots of animals on the quilt, maybe even a teddy bear.

Yvette relaxes in her apartment.

It is important to see people with HIV as human beings and not be terrified. Many people have it and are healthy. They live good lives. HIV is not necessarily a death sentence.

But a little fear is healthy. There is healthy fear and reactive fear. Healthy fear is when you are informed and know there is a possibility of catching or transmitting the virus to someone else. You take responsibility for your behavior. An unhealthy fear is when you are not informed; you are not sure how you get it. You are just reacting with fear of the possibility. If you don't ask questions, you remain ignorant and have unjustified fears. That can be scary because you are living in a world where you are not sure. Take measures to protect yourself. If more people did that, it would slow the transmission of the virus. It is at the point now where it is not going to go away.

Finally, don't make the same mistakes I did. Take action. Have compassion. Fight AIDS. Don't be afraid to be with someone with AIDS. Give them a smile. Give them a hug.

CHAPTER 10

REMEMBER
THEIR
NAMES

THE STORY OF AIDS IS NOT JUST BIOLOGY —VIRUSES, vaccines, and immune systems. It's about real lives snuffed out in their prime. It's about suffering and sorrow. It's about courage, compassion, and commitment. It's about loved ones left behind asking why.

To celebrate life and remember the goodness of those that have gone, there is a memorial to those no longer with us. The memorial is not stone or statue. The memorial is in the form of a quilt—the Names Project. It is a symbol of love and remembrance.

Each memorial panel is a three-foot-by-six-foot quilt. Each is a loving commemoration. For those who made the panels, it is a way to say, "You will not be forgotten." Sets of these quilts are sewn together and displayed on the ground with fabric walkways around them.

First created in 1987, in a small storefront in San Francisco, the project is now international in scope. The first display in San Francisco, on June 28, 1987, had 40 panels. By the

This aerial view shows the AIDS quilt displayed on the National Mall in Washington, D.C. The Names Project is a memorial in the form of a quilt to those who have died from AIDS.

time of the quilt's first display in Washington, D.C., in October 1987, there were 1,920 panels on display, covering an area equal to two football fields. A year later that number had risen to 8,288 panels.

By 1992, the AIDS Memorial Quilt had panels from every U.S. state and 20 countries. By 1996, 40 countries were represented, truly reflecting the global nature of the AIDS pandemic.

As of July 1996, the quilt had 36,199 panels, with more arriving every day. If completely displayed, it would take up 21 football fields. Each quilt has been sewn together by friends, lovers, or family members. Each panel is a unique piece of art, capturing a small essence of a life lost to AIDS. For most, the sewing is not the hard part. It is reliving the memories and the dreams that are most difficult.

Most panels honor a single person, but some remember a parent and child or two lovers or a group of friends. For those making a quilt, it is an important part of the grieving process. It is a major investment in time, love, creativity, and emotion. Panels often contain photos, poems, letters, and diaries telling stories of love and loss. Sewn into quilts are toys, clothes, flags, ribbons, signs, buttons, and awards. All have special meaning and special memories. They help piece together a life.

The experience of seeing the quilt has been shared by more than 7 million people. It's moving, uplifting, and sobering. The experience is hard to describe, but it is like doing three things at the same time—going to a picnic, a funeral, and an art gallery. If you can imagine all the emotions evoked by these three types of events—all wrapped up in one—then you have some idea of what it feels like to view the quilt.

A typical outdoor quilt viewing begins at sunrise. Hours before, volunteers have laid down the material walkway grid. Openings in the grid are left where each 12-foot-by-12-foot panel of eight quilts will be unfolded by teams of eight volunteers. The folded panels open "like the petals of a flower." They are then lifted and rotated into place on the opening in the walkway. Once on the ground, the panel is attached to the walkway by plastic ties.

Throughout the day, the names of those who have died and whose panels are on display are read by volunteers. In various locations throughout the quilt grid are blank panels. People can write messages and thoughts on the blank panels.

When the quilt comes to your area, volunteer to help. You might want to form a committee to start such a project. The National Names Project will help you with what you need to do. People are always needed to set up the walkways, open the quilts, read names, comfort those in need of support, provide security, serve food, and collect donations for AIDS-related causes.

Helping as a volunteer or making a quilt is a meaningful thing to do. It is a good way to get involved in HIV awareness.

How to Make a Quilt

Making a quilt is a great project for a class, group of friends, community-minded individuals, or those wanting to remember a special person.

Base Materials
The base quilt material should be a strong fabric. A medium-weight, nonstretch fabric, such as cotton or poplin, works best. It needs to hold up to sewing, folding, shipping, and being displayed on the ground or hung on a wall, if necessary. A backing fabric is recommended. It helps retain the shape of the quilt and keeps the panel clean when displayed on the ground.

Size

The finished quilt needs to be three feet by six feet. This includes all borders and seams. Cut the fabric about three inches larger on all sides so you can fold over a hem and sew it in place. This will keep the fabric from fraying.

Getting Help

An important decision is whether to make the quilt yourself or work with a group of friends or relatives. Working with others, like an old-fashioned quilting bee, can be fun and supportive of each in the group, especially if all of you knew the person who died of AIDS.

Design

Do not worry about artistic achievement. Make your panel for a single person, using at least a first name. Using the whole name is best. If the person was a doctor or nurse or other professional, put the appropriate designation (M.D. or R.N., for example) after their name. Those letters tell important things about a person.

Think about the person. What were their hobbies and habits? What about their profession, schooling, travel, likes, hometown, religion, friends and family, and favorite sports, food, colors, clothes, cars, or places? How will you represent some of these things on the quilt? Pick those that are most significant.

Put your ideas down on paper. Experiment with different designs. It can be horizontal or vertical. Make sketches of your different ideas and designs. Put the sketches up on a bulletin board. Leave them there for a while to see how you like them. For the ones you think you like best, make a quarter-scale drawing (9 inches by 18 inches). Then finally, with the one you like, make a full-scale drawing.

Think about colors. Your choices may have a special significance. How do the colors look with the other things you

This quilt section from the Names Project shows a variety of designs. Making a quilt is a great project for groups and individuals.

are putting on the quilt? You might want to try your design with several different color combinations.

Construction

If you are going to put items, such as pictures or toys, on the quilt, place them on the full-scale drawing and see how they fit. Make sure they are flat and do not stick up. Heavy items are not good because they come off easily.

Cut out letters and sew them to the background. For slippery fabric, like satin, glue them down first, then sew them in place. Precut letters are available, but their adhesive does not stay well, so they must be sewn down. Anything glued on must also be sewn because glue breaks down over time. Glitter and sequins do not stay in place, so do not use them.

Textile paints, color-fast dyes, or indelible markers can be used for designs or lettering. Designs and letters will be sharper and clearer if you make a stencil first and then color it in.

Photos can be duplicated on iron-on transfers and then ironed onto the quilt. These transfers work best if the background is a light color and the background fabric is either cotton or a cotton-polyester blend.

Remember the quilt will be folded and unfolded many times. Durability of the design and construction is very important. Make sure things will not crack or fall off during folding.

If you are sending the quilt to the Names Project, it should be mailed to 310 Townsend Street, Suite 310, San Francisco, CA 94107. Phone: 415-882-5500. Fax: 415-882-6200. Along with the quilt, send a photo of the person, if possible, and a one- or two-page letter about the person. Include hometown, special things you remember, your relationship to the person, and other information you would like in the project's archives. *Call before sending a quilt panel.*

Once they receive your panel, volunteers check it for

Young people view the AIDS quilt in Washington, D.C.

size and durability. If necessary, it's adjusted for size, reinforcement, or minor repairs. Next, it is stored geographically by region. When eight panels from the same region are collected, they are sewn together in a twelve-foot square. This now becomes a block of the quilt that gets a reference number. You can always find out where your panel is being displayed by using that reference number. You can also request that it be displayed at a certain location in your area if the quilt is on display.

For further information check out the Names Project web site: http:/www.aidsquilt.org/

EPILOGUE

MANY THINGS HAVE BEEN DISCUSSED IN THIS BOOK.
Hopefully, they have been helpful in answering your questions about HIV and AIDS. If you have further questions, take the time to call the hot lines or search the web sites on the Internet listed in the reference section.

Here are some of the most important things to remember:

1. HIV infection is preventable.

2. You may not know when you or your partner has HIV infection because symptoms are not always noticeable.

3. Anyone who is sexually involved should have regular medical checkups.

4. Barrier methods (condoms, dental dams) with spermicides can reduce the risk of getting HIV

infection, but only sexual abstinence can prevent it 100 percent of the time.

5. The use of alcohol and drugs influence your involvement in risk behaviors for HIV infection.

6. There is no cure, vaccine, or immunity to HIV infection or AIDS.

Above all, treat people with respect. You can learn many lessons by giving of yourself and helping those in need of love, care, and understanding. Take the time to volunteer. Raise money, counsel, deliver food, or just be there for someone who is HIV positive. Remember to smile, to listen, and to embrace. Simple acts of kindness will transform pain into compassion.

Too many people pretend that AIDS is something that happens to others, in other cities, to other people who use drugs, who are gay, who are poor, or who are different. But HIV infection is an equal-opportunity disease. If you ignore it, if you do not think about prevention, it will be part of your life also. Don't let this happen to you.

Learn the facts, be a beacon of strength, and stand up for what is right for you. Talk to your partner and friends and practice the lowest level of risk-taking behavior that is acceptable for you.

Good luck in educating yourself and your very special friends.

SOURCE NOTES

Chapter 1

1. "Current Trends Update: Acquired Immunodeficiency Syndrome—United States," *Morbidity and Mortality Weekly Report*, 35: 49 (December 12, 1986).
2. " Update: Trends in AIDS Incidence, Deaths, and Prevalence—United States, 1996." *Morbidity and Mortality Weekly Report*, 46: 8 (February 28, 1997).

Chapter 4

1. Webster, A., "HIV Is a Mind/Body Issue," The Mind-Body Medical Clinic for HIV-Positive and AIDS Related Disorders, Beth Israel/Deacones Medical Center, Harvard Medical School, Boston, MA, 1996.

Chapter 5

1. Studies performed at the CDC have shown that drying HIV causes, within several hours, a 90 percent to 99 percent reduction of HIV concentration. These studies were done with fluids that had HIV concentrations of at least 100,000 times greater than typically found in infected blood or semen. "Guidelines for Prevention of Transmission of Human Immunodeficiency Virus and Hepatitis B Virus to Health-Care and Public-Safety Workers,"

Centers for Disease Control and Prevention, February 1989, p. 40.

2. In July 1997, one case of possible transmission between a known HIV-infected man and his previously uninfected female sex partner became public. They had engaged in regular "deep kissings" as well as sexual intercourse. Because they had bad dental habits and deep gingivitis, the deep kissing was highly suspect as the mode of transmission, but other modes could not be ruled out. "Transmission of HIV Possibly Associated with Exposure of Mucous Membrane to Contaminated Blood," *Morbidity and Mortality Weekly Report*, July 11, 1997.

3. Men having sex with men (51 percent) plus heterosexual cases (8 percent) for a total of 67 percent. Note, there were an additional 7 percent of all cases that had multiple risks, including sex. Centers for Disease Control and Prevention, "HIV/AIDS Surveillance Report," 8:1 (November 1, 1996).

4. "AIDS Associated with Injecting-Drug Use," *Morbidity and Mortality Weekly Report*, 45: 19 (May 17, 1995).

5. Needle exchange programs have been shown to be extremely effective in reducing the spread of HIV. Not only are old needles exchanged for clean ones, but addicts are encouraged to get into treatment and counseling. Most programs also distribute needle-cleaning kits and help users take better care of themselves. They do not encourage drug use, do not exchange needles on the street, and do not give out needles unless a used one is exchanged.

Chapter 8

1. This has been shown to be true in at least three studies: (1) A. Saracco, M. Musicco, A. Nicolosi, et al., "Man-to-Woman Sexual Transmission of HIV: Longitudinal

Study of 343 Steady Partners of Infected Men," *Journal of Acquired Immune Deficiency Syndrome*, Vol. 6 (1993): 497–502; (2) J. Trussell, R.A. Hatcher, W. Cotes, F. H. Stewart, and K. Kost, "Contraceptive Failures in the United States: An Update," *Studies in Family Planning*, 21 (1991): 51–54; and (3) P. Van dePerre, D. Jacobs, S. Sprecher-Goldberger, "The Latex Condom, an Efficient Barrier Against Sexual Transmission of AIDS-Related Virus," *AIDS*, 1 (1987): 49–52.

GLOSSARY

abstinence — saying no, not doing something; usually refers to not having *sexual intercourse* or not using drugs

acquired immunodeficiency syndrome (AIDS) — the end stage of *HIV* infection, an incurable *disease* caused by the HIV virus

acupuncture — the Chinese practice of piercing specific nerves with needles to reduce discomfort

addiction — a compulsive need for a habit-forming substance; there are physiological and psychological *symptoms*

AIDS — see *acquired immunodeficiency syndrome*

antibiotic — a substance produced or derived from a microorganism and able to inhibit or kill another microorganism

antibody — a *protein* made by the body's *B cells* to help fight infection

antigen — a *bacteria, virus,* or other foreign substance that causes the body to form an *antibody*

antivirals — compounds that are effective in treating *virus* infections

assay — a chemical solution that is used to determine the presence of a certain substance in a fluid

asymptomatic — a time during a *disease* when a person is infected but shows no *symptoms*

attenuated virus — a weakened *virus* used to make a *vaccine*

autologous transfusion — when a person receives their own blood donated several weeks before surgery

AZT — azidothymidine; an antiviral drug marketed under the name Retrovir®; prolongs the life of *HIV* patients by interfering with the genetic replication of the *virus*

bacteria — one-celled organisms, some of which cause *disease*

B cell — a white blood cell that makes antibodies to fight infection

blood bank — a place where blood is stored until it is needed for *transfusion*

blood donor — a person who gives some of his or her blood to a *blood bank* or hospital

blood transfusion — a process by which one person receives blood from another person

blood typing — matching one person's blood with another person's blood to see if it is compatible for *transfusion*

cofactor — something that increases the speed at which a *disease* develops

condom, male — a special balloonlike sheath that can be placed over a man's penis before *sexual intercourse*; it can prevent the spread of *disease* and keep his female partner from becoming pregnant

cytokine — chemicals secreted from cells that signal messages to other cells

dementia — a gradual loss of mental function due to organic *disease* or brain injury; an *opportunistic infection* for those with *AIDS*

dental dam — a flat sheet of latex placed over the vagina to prevent the spread of disease during oral sex

disease — a group of physical problems caused by an organism or the degeneration of a body part

DNA — deoxyribonucleic acid; a double strand of genetic material, composed of paired nitrogenous bases, that contain the genetic codes for an organism's inherited characteristics

drug abuser — a person who uses drugs to change the way he or she feels, not to make themselves well

ELISA test — a blood test for antibodies of *HIV*; the test shows whether a person's blood has been infected with HIV; results are sometimes a *false positive*; it is usually confirmed with the *Western blot* test

enzyme — any of a group of *proteins* produced by living cells that induce chemical reactions in living things

epidemiologist — a scientist who studies the spread of *disease*

Epstein-Barr virus — one of the *herpes viruses* that causes mononucleosis and a type of *lymphoma*

gay — a homosexual; usually refers to a male (see *lesbian*)

genital warts — a sexually transmitted *disease* caused by a *virus*; warts form on the penis, around the vagina, and around the anus

gonorrhea — a sexually transmitted *disease* caused by the gonococcus *bacteria*; can cause sterility

hemophilia — an *inherited disease* that causes internal bleeding and makes people unable to stop bleeding when cut or bruised; mainly affects men

hemophiliac — a person with *hemophilia*

hepatitis — an inflammation of the liver, usually caused by a *virus*; often produces a yellow color to the eyes and skin; there are different types of hepatitis: hepatitis A, B, C, D, and E

herpes virus — a family of *viruses*, including herpes simplex, that cause painful sores on the mouth (simplex I) or anus and genital area (simplex II), herpes zoster, cytomegalovirus, and *Epstein-Barr virus*; these *diseases* are more persistent in people with AIDS

heterogeneity — the ability of a cell to alter its look or surface structure; *HIV* cells use this ability to prevent detection by the immune system

heterosexual — a person who prefers a member of the opposite sex for romantic or sexual relations

HIV — an abbreviation for human immunodeficiency virus, the *virus* that causes *HIV* infection and *AIDS* (used to be called HTLV-III and LAV)

HIV-2 — causes an *HIV* infection-like *disease*; a different organism from HIV

homosexual — a person whose sexual orientation is toward members of the same gender

immune system — the body's defense system for fighting *viruses, bacteria,* and other outside threats; *lymph glands* and T cells and B cells that protect you from infections

infection — an invasion by organisms such as *bacteria, viruses,* or fungi

inherited disease — a *disease* that a person is born with, caused by genetic defect

intravenous — injected inside a vein

IV drugs — drugs taken by injecting them into one's veins

Kaposi's sarcoma — cancer of the walls of the blood and lymphatic vessels; usually appears as pink and purple painless spots on the skin but may also occur on internal organs; an *opportunistic infection* for those with AIDS

lesbian — a female homosexual

lymph glands — glands located in various parts of the body that filter microorganisms out of the lymph fluid and produce lymphocytes

lymphoma — cancer of the lymphocytes (*B cells*) of the *immune system*

monocyte — a type of white blood cell that engulfs and destroys *bacteria* and other disease-producing organisms

monogamous — having sexual relations with only one person over a long period of time

mutation — a change in the genetic material of cell or a *virus*

nonoxynol-9 — a *spermicide* that also kills *HIV*; frequently used with *condoms* for more complete *disease* prevention

opportunistic infection — *disease* caused by germs that would ordinarily be destroyed by the *immune system*

oral thrush candida — a disease that occurs in the mouth; characterized by white patches on the tongue or inside the cheeks

outercourse — a term used as a synonym for *safe sex*

pandemic — an outbreak of infectious *disease* that spreads rapidly through the population affecting large numbers of people in many countries

pathogen — anything that causes *disease*, such as a *virus, bacteria, yeast,* or *protozoan*

Pneumocystis carinii pneumonia — a type of pneumonia, or inflammation of the lungs, caused by a *protozoan*; often called PCP; an *opportunistic infection* for those with AIDS

polymerase chain reaction (PCR) test — a diagnostic test that identifies *HIV* by finding HIV *DNA*

protein — a compound in the body and in food that is necessary for growth and functioning

protozoans — large one-celled microorganisms that can cause *diseases*

retrovirus — a *virus* containing *RNA* as its genetic materials; has the ability to create an image of the host *DNA*; usually RNA is created from DNA, therefore this is the reverse, or retroprocess; this DNA can combine with the DNA of the host cell and allow the virus to reproduce; *HIV* is a retrovirus

reverse transcriptase — an *enzyme* that allows the retrovirus that produced it to make a *DNA* copy of its *RNA*

RNA — ribonucleic acid; a single strand of genetic material composed of paired nitrogenous bases

safe sex — nonpenetrative sexual behavior that does not expose one to another individual's blood, *semen, vaginal secretions,* or breast milk on or near the anus, vagina, mouth, urethra or into an opening on the skin

safer sex — oral, anal, or vaginal intercourse with a properly used *condom*

semen — a body fluid that contains sperm and male reproductive fluids; expelled from the penis during sexual activity

seroconversion — the time when the body begins to produce *antibodies* in response to an *antigen* invasion

seroconversion window — the time from *infection* by an *antigen* and the time that a test can detect the presence of *antibodies*

seropositive — a condition in which *antibodies* to a particular disease-producing organism are found in the blood

sexual contact — touching, kissing, or intercourse between two people for sexual pleasure

sexual intercourse — the entry of the man's penis into the vagina, mouth, or anus of his sexual partner

sexually transmitted disease (STD) — one of many *diseases* that is transmitted during *sexual intercourse*

sign — evidence of a *disease* that a physician or other health care worker can detect; for example, high blood pressure, fever, and swelling

spermicide — a substance that kills sperm cells; used in the form of creams, jellies, and foams with a diaphragm or *condom* as a contraceptive; *nonoxynol-9* also kills *HIV* when used in conjunction with a condom

stress — the body's physical, mental, and emotional reaction — for example, headaches, high blood pressure, pain, ulcers—to what is happening in your environment

stress management — skills to identify and reduce the harmful effects of stressors in your life

stressors — things in one's environment that cause stress, such as bills, job, school, and not enough time

symptom — subjective evidence of *disease* that a patient feels; for example, headache or toothache

syncytia — multinucleated masses of *CD4* cells; this results in the destruction of those CD4 cells; it is formed by cells hooking together

syndrome — a groups of *signs* and *symptoms* that occur together and indicate that someone has a certain *disease*

T cell — white blood cell that can recognize invaders that cause illness; *T cells* alert *B cells* and instruct them to produce *antibodies*

toxoplasmosis — a *disease* caused by the toxoplasma organism that lives within the cells of a host; an *opportunistic infection* for those with AIDS, usually affecting brain cells; comes from raw or undercooked meat or cat feces

transfusion — the transfer of a liquid, such as blood or saline, into the bloodstream

transmission — the process of spreading an organism

twelve-step program — a self-help program that guides a person through specific stages toward their recovery; programs may focus on alcoholism, drug abuse, gambling, and other serious problems

unsafe sex — oral, anal, or vaginal *sexual intercourse* without a *condom*

vaccine — a substance usually made of killed or weakened *bacteria* or *virus*, usually an injection, given to people to prevent a *disease*

vaginal secretions — fluid excreted from the vagina

virus — a tiny parasite composed of genetic material and a *protein* coat; they must destroy the host cell to reproduce

Western blot — blood test for *antibodies* to *HIV*; is more specific than the *ELISA test*; performed to confirm a positive ELISA test

works — drug injecting equipment used to inject drugs below the surface of the skin; includes needles, cooker, cotton, and string or elastic

FOR FURTHER INFORMATION

Books

Burns, Janice. *Sarah's Song*. New York: Warner Books, 1995. An informative true story that puts a face to AIDS.

Callen, M., ed. *Surviving and Thriving with AIDS: Hints for the Newly Diagnosed*. New York: People with AIDS Coalition, 1987. A collection of essays and articles by persons with AIDS that presents a wide variety of experiences and opinions.

Peabody, B. *The Screaming Room: A Mother's Journal of Her Son's Struggle with AIDS—A True Story of Love, Dedication, and Courage*. New York: Avon Books, 1986. A personal and moving story of what it is like to care for someone who is ill.

Shilts, Randy. *And the Band Played On: Politics, People, and the AIDS Epidemic*. New York: St. Martin's Press, 1987. A chronicle of the politics and events of the early years of the epidemic.

Films and Videos

And the Band Played On.
Home Box Office Inc., 1100 Avenue of Americas, New York, N.Y. 10036 (212-512-1000).

This feature film chronicles the AIDS epidemic from the first reported cases through 1993. The story is told from the perspective of Dr. Don Francis, a researcher from CDC. The film highlights the interactions and conflict between Francis, researchers at the Pasteur Institute, and Dr. Robert Gallo of the National Institutes of Health. The early struggle to mandate testing and screening for all blood donors is depicted.

Philadelphia.
Columbia Tristar Home Video, 3400 Riverside Drive,
Burbank, CA 91505

This 1993 feature film is the story of a lawyer with AIDS who sues his former employer, a prestigious law firm, for AIDS discrimination.

Web Sites

AIDS Now! For Teens
http://www.itec.sfsu.edu/aids.html

This site provides answers to students' questions about AIDS.

The National Names Project
http://www.aidsquilt.org/

This site contains general information on the quilt, locations for display, how to make a quilt and submit it to the Names Project and updated general information on HIV infection and AIDS. Here are other ways to contact the Names Project: 10 Townsend St. Suite 310, San Francisco, CA 94107-1639. Phone: 415-882-5500. Fax: 415-882-6200. E-mail: info@aidsquilt.org

Go Ask Alice!
http://www.columbia.edu/cu/healthwise

A service of the Healthwise University Health Service at New York City's Columbia University, this site answers health-related questions from college students at Columbia

University. All the past questions and answers are archived on the web site. You can search the questions and read the answers. They are catalogued by question type. Included are such topics as general health, sexual health, AIDS, nutrition, disease prevention, and relationships. A good source of honest up-to-date information.

The Body
http://www.thebody.com/index.html

This site, sponsored by Body Health Resources Corporation, has good information on a variety of HIV-related topics, including prevention, treatments, drug therapy, and vaccines.

Project Inform
http://www.projinf.org/

This site has up-to-date information on medication and treatments for HIV and opportunistic infections. You can also reach Project Inform at 1965 Market Street, Suite 220, San Francisco, CA 94103. Phone: 415-558- 8669. Fax: 415-558-0684.

San Diego Clean Needle Exchange
http://www.wilder.net/sus/needle.htm

This site describes the San Diego County program and has an excellent list of other web sites for further information on needle-exchange programs, including recent reports, literature, and research. You can also contact them at P.O. Box 4821, San Diego, CA 92164-4821. Phone: 619-645-0523. E-mail: wbrent@ix.netcom.com.

National Hot Lines for
Information or Help

HIV Treatment and Medication
Hotline 1-800-822-7422

Home Testing Hotline 1-800-HIV-TEST

National AIDS Hotline 1-800-342-2437
    TTY Line 1-800-234-7889
    Spanish-language line 1-800-344-7432

National AIDS Treatment Hotline ...1-800-448-0440

National Pediatric HIV
Resource Center 1-800-362-0071

National AIDS Information
Clearinghouse 1-800-458-5231

National Clearinghouse for Alcohol
and Drug Information 1-800-729-6686

Teens and AIDS Hotline 1-800-234-TEEN

Calls to all of these hot lines are toll free.

INDEX

Page numbers in *italics* indicate illustrations.

Abstinence, 93–96, *97*, 142
Acquired immune deficiency syndrome (AIDS), 13, 25, 43–48, 129, 131, 142
AIDS dementia, 46, 53, 56
AIDS Memorial Quilt, 129, 132–40, *133*, *137*, *139*
Acupuncture, 85
Africa, 13–14, 15, 18, 19, 39
Alternative therapies, 85–88
Amino acids, 91
Anal intercourse, 61, 62–63, 93, 111. *See also* Safer sex, Safe sex
Anemia, 52
Antibiotics, 22
Antibodies, 26, 29, 30, 31, 32, 33, 50, 71, 72, 76, 91
Antigens, 26, 28, 29, 72, 90
Antiviral medications, 78–83, *80*
Aroma therapy, 88
Asymptomatic stage, 32, 43, 45, 49
Australia, 18
Autologous transfusions, 24
AZT, 49, 77, 81, 82, 128, 129

B cells, 26, *27*, 28, 29, 32, 56
Bisexuality, 17, 18, 19
Blood-brain barrier, 81
Blood-clotting factor, 23
Blood supply, 22–24, *23*, 67, 71, 75
Blood transfusions, 16, 17, 18, 22–24, 50, 92
Blood typing, 22
Bone marrow, 32, 55
Bone marrow cells, 30
Bovine immunodeficiency virus (BIV), 40
Bovine leukemia virus (BLV), 40

Bubonic plague, 19–20

Cancer, 14, 32
    cervical, *47*, 48, 56
Candidiasis, *47*, 48, *86*
Capsid protein (p24), 37, 91
Caribbean, the, 13–14, 18
CD4 cell counts, 48, 49–50, 81, 82, *84*
CD4 receptor sites, 28, 30–33, 37, 57, 63, 66, 78–79
Centers for Disease Control and Prevention (CDC), 14, 17, 58
Central nervous system, 32
Cerebrospinal fluid, 81
Children with HIV. *See* Pediatric HIV
Cholera, 21
Cigarettes, 45
Circumcision, 64–65
Cofactors, 45–46
Colon cells, 30
Columnar epithelial cells, 63
Condoms, 17, 66, 93, 98, 101, 102–11, *103*, *105*, *107*, *112*, 121, 141
Contraceptives, 66
Core protein, 37–39
Cryptococcosis, *47*, *86*
Cryptosporidiosis, 55, *86*
Cytokines, 29, 32, 33
Cytomegalovirus (CMV), *47*, 54, *86*

ddC, 82
ddI, 81–82
Dendritic cells, 28, 29, 30
Dental dams, 98, 101, 111, 141
d4T, 82
Diabetics, 68, 72
Diarrhea, 44, 49, 52, 55, 81, 85
DNA, 31, 35, 37, 39, 52, 74

157 ▼

Early HIV infection stage, 42–43
ELISA test, 72, 73
Envelope, the, 34, 35, 37, 39
Epstein-Barr virus, 54, 56
Europe, 18, 21
Exercise, 87

False negative results, 72, 75
False positive results, 72, 75
Feline immunodeficiency virus
    (FIV), 40
Feline leukemia virus (FeLV), 40
Female condoms, 110–11, *110,*
    123–24

Gay related immune disorder
    (GRID), 14
Gonorrhea, 64, 93
gp 120, 30, 35, 37, 91
Guided imagery, 87

Hairy Leukoplakia, 54
Haiti, 14
Helper T cells, 28, 30, 32
Hemophiliacs, 16, 17, 18, 23–24, 45
Hepatitis, 22, 24, 113
Hepatitis B, 24, 113
Hepatitis C, 24
Heterogeneity, 31
Heterosexuality, 17, 18, 19, 48, 62,
    64–66, 68
Histoplasmosis, *47*
Home testing kits, 71, 73
Human immunodeficiency virus
    (HIV)
    and the immune system,
        25–33, 45, 46, 49, 50, 54,
        56, 64, 72, 127, 128, 132
    medications for, 78–83, 127
    nature of, 34–56, *36, 38*
    origins of, 13–24, 40
    prevention of, 92–115
    testing, 71–77
    transmission of, 57–70

HIV-1. *See* Human immunodefi-
    ciency virus (HIV)
HIV-2, 39, 71
HIV wasting syndrome, 46, *47,* 52,
    85
Human T-cell Lymphotropic virus
    (HTLV-I), 13, 71
Human T-cell Lymphotropic virus
    (HTLV-II), 71
Human T-cell Lymphotropic virus
    HTLV-III, 13, 16
Hypnosis, 87
Hysteria, 15, *15,* 17, 20, 21, 131

Immune globulin, 23
Immune system, 25–33, 45, 46, 49,
    50, 54, 56, 64, 72, 127, 128,
    132
Indinivar, 83
Inducer T cells, 28
Influenza, 21
Inner shell, the, 37
Integrase enzymes, 37
Intravenous drug use, 15, 17, 19,
    24, 43, 45, 48, 68–70, 92, 93,
    95, 96, 113–15, 118, 122–23,
    124–25. *See also* Needles,
    contaminated

Kaposi's sarcoma, 14, *47,* 56

Lymphadenopathy-associated
    virus (LAV), 16
Lymphoma, *47,* 56

Macrophage cells, 28, 29, 30, 32
Massage, 86–87
Matrix protein (p17), 37
M Cells, 29
Memory cells, 26, 29, 30
Monkeys, 13, 39–40
Monocyte cells, 28, 30
Montagnier, Luc, 16
Mosquitoes, 61

About the Author

Kenneth L. Packer has taught health and AIDS education on all grade levels and has coordinated health-education programs for several school districts. He has also been the executive director of a local Heart Association chapter and has worked with many community-based organizations on a variety of health topics, including HIV prevention. He is the author of a health-education textbook and a book about puberty for middle-school students and has written many local and state health education curriculum guides.

Mr. Packer is the former AIDS Education Coordinator for the Lower Hudson Valley in New York State and directed a Regional Health Education Center at BOCES, in Yorktown Heights, New York. Presently, he is a consultant conducting teacher and community training and student workshops on health topics, including health education and HIV prevention.